DODGE VIPER
PERFORMANCE PORTFOLIO
1990-1998

Compiled by R M Clarke

ISBN 1 85520 472X

BROOKLANDS BOOKS LTD.
P.O. BOX 146, COBHAM,
SURREY, KT11 1LG. UK

Brooklands Books

MOTORING

BROOKLANDS ROAD TEST SERIES

Abarth Gold Portfolio 1950-1971
AC Ace & Aceca 1953-1983
Alfa Romeo Giulietta Gold Portfolio 1954-1965
Alfa Romeo Giulia Coupés 1963-1976
Alfa Romeo Giulia Coupés Gold Port. 1963-1976
Alfa Romeo Spider 1966-1990
Alfa Romeo Spider Gold Portfolio 1966-1991
Alfa Romeo Alfasud 1972-1984
Alfa Romeo Alfetta Gold Portfolio 1972-1987
Alfa Romeo Alfetta GTV6 1980-1986
Allard Gold Portfolio 1937-1959
Alvis Gold Portfolio 1919-1967
AMX & Javelin Muscle Portfolio 1968-1974
Armstrong Siddeley Gold Portfolio 1945-1960
Aston Martin Gold Portfolio 1948-1971
Aston Martin Gold Portfolio 1972-1985
Aston Martin Gold Portfolio 1985-1995
Audi Quattro Gold Portfolio 1980-1991
Austin A30 & A35 1951-1962
Austin Healey 100 & 100/6 Gold Portfolio 1952-1959
Austin Healey 3000 Gold Portfolio 1959-1967
Austin Healey Sprite Gold Portfolio 1958-1971
BMW 6 & 8 Cyl. Cars Limited Edition 1935-1960
BMW 1600 Collection No.1 1966-1981
BMW 2002 Gold Portfolio 1968-1976
BMW 6 Cylinder Coupés & Saloons Gold P. 1969-1976
BMW 316, 318, 320 (4 cyl.) Gold Port. 1975-1990
BMW 320, 323, 325 (6 cyl.) Gold Port. 1977-1990
BMW M Series Gold Portfolio 1976-1997
BMW 5 Series Gold Portfolio 1981-1987
BMW 6 Series Gold Portfolio 1976-1989
Bricklin Gold Portfolio 1974-1975
Bristol Cars Gold Portfolio 1946-1992
Buick Automobiles 1947-1960
Buick Muscle Cars 1965-1970
Cadillac Allanté 1986-1993
Cadillac Automobiles 1949-1959
Cadillac Automobiles 1960-1969
Checker Limited Edition
Chevrolet 1955-1957
Impala & SS Muscle Portfolio 1958-1972
Corvair Performance Portfolio 1959-1969
El Camino & SS Muscle Portfolio 1959-1987
Chevy II & Nova SS Muscle Portfolio 1962-1974
Chevelle & SS Muscle Portfolio 1964-1972
Caprice Limited Edition 1965-1976
Chevrolet Muscle Cars 1966-1971
Chevy Blazer 1969-1981
Camaro Muscle Portfolio 1967-1973
Chevrolet Camaro & Z-28 1973-1981
High Performance Camaros 1982-1988
Chevrolet Corvette Gold Portfolio 1953-1962
Chevrolet Corvette Sting Ray Gold Port. 1963-1967
Chevrolet Corvette Gold Portfolio 1968-1977
High Performance Corvettes 1983-1989
Chrysler 300 Gold Portfolio 1955-1970
Imperial Limited Edition 1955-1970
Valiant 1960-1962
Citroen Traction Avant Gold Portfolio 1934-1957
Citroen 2CV Gold Portfolio 1948-1989
Citroen DS & ID 1955-1975
Citroen DS & ID Gold Portfolio 1955-1975
Citroen SM 1970-1975
Cobras & Replicas 1962-1983
Shelby Cobra Gold Portfolio 1962-1969
Cobras & Cobra Replicas Gold Portfolio 1962-1989
Crosley & Crosley Specials Limited Edition
Cunningham Automobiles 1951-1955
Daimler SP250 Sports & V-8 250 Saloon Gold P. 1959-1969
Datsun Roadsters 1962-1971
Datsun 240Z & 260Z Gold Portfolio 1970-1978
Datsun 280Z & ZX 1975-1983
DeLorean Gold Portfolio 1977-1995
De Soto Limited Edition 1952-1960
Charger Muscle Portfolio 1966-1974
Dodge Muscle Cars 1967-1970
Dodge Viper Performance Portfolio 1990-1998
ERA Gold Portfolio 1934-1994
Excalibur Collection No.1 1952-1981
Facel Vega 1954-1964
Ferrari Limited Edition 1947-1957
Ferrari Limited Edition 1958-1963
Ferrari Dino 1965-1974
Ferrari Dino 308 & Mondial Gold Portfolio 1974-1985
Ferrari 328 348 Mondial Gold Portfolio 1986-1994
Fiat 500 Gold Portfolio 1936-1972
Fiat 600 & 850 Gold Portfolio 1955-1972
Fiat Pininfarina 124 & 2000 Spider 1968-1985
Fiat X1/9 Gold Portfolio 1973-1989
Fiat Abarth Performance Portfolio 1972-1987
Ford Consul, Zephyr, Zodiac Mk. I & II 1950-1962
Ford Zephyr, Zodiac, Executive Mk. III & IV 1962-1971
Ford Cortina 1600E & GT 1967-1970
High Performance Capris Gold Portfolio 1969-1987
Capri Muscle Portfolio 1974-1987
High Performance Fiestas 1979-1991
High Performance Escorts Mk. I 1968-1974
High Performance Escorts Mk. II 1975-1980
High Performance Escorts 1980-1985
High Performance Escorts 1985-1990
High Perf. Sierras & Merkurs Gold Portfolio 1983-1990
Ford Automobiles 1949-1959
Ford Fairlane Performance Portfolio 1955-1970
Ford Ranchero Performance Portfolio 1957-1979
Edsel Limited Edition 1957-1960
Falcon Performance Portfolio 1960-1970
Ford Galaxie & LTD Limited Edition 1960-1973
Ford Thunderbird 1955-1957
Ford Thunderbird 1958-1963
Ford GT40 Gold Portfolio 1964-1987
Ford Torino Limited Edition 1968-1974
Ford Bronco 1966-1977
Ford Bronco 1978-1988
Goggomobil Limited Edition
Holden 1948-1962
Honda CRX 1983-1987
Hudson Limited Edition 1946-1957
International Scout Gold Portfolio 1961-1980
Isetta Gold Portfolio 1953-1964
ISO & Bizzarrini Gold Portfolio 1962-1974
Jaguar and SS Gold Portfolio 1931-1951
Jaguar C-Type & D-Type Gold Portfolio 1951-1960
Jaguar XK120, 140, 150 Gold Portfolio 1948-1960
Jaguar Mk. VII, VIII, IX, X, 420 Gold Port. 1950-1970
Jaguar Mk. 1 & Mk. 2 Gold Portfolio 1959-1969
Jaguar E-Type Gold Portfolio 1961-1971
Jaguar E-Type V-12 1971-1975
Jaguar S-Type & 420 Limited Edition
Jaguar XJ12, XJ5.3, V12 Gold Portfolio 1972-1990
Jaguar XJ6 Series I & II Gold Portfolio 1968-1979
Jaguar XJ6 Series III Perf. Portfolio 1979-1986
Jaguar XJ6 Gold Portfolio 1986-1994
Jaguar XJS Gold Portfolio 1975-1988
Jaguar XJS Gold Portfolio 1988-1995
Jaguar XK8 Limited Edition
Jeep CJ5 & CJ6 1960-1976
Jeep CJ5 & CJ7 1976-1986
Jensen Interceptor Gold Portfolio 1966-1986
Jensen Healey 1972-1976
Kaiser - Frazer Limited Edition 1946-1955
Lagonda Gold Portfolio 1919-1964
Lancia Aurelia & Flaminia Gold Portfolio 1950-1970
Lancia Fulvia Gold Portfolio 1963-1976
Lancia Beta Gold Portfolio 1972-1984
Lancia Delta Gold Portfolio 1979-1994
Lancia Stratos 1972-1985
Land Rover Series I 1948-1958
Land Rover Series II & IIa 1958-1971
Land Rover 90 110 Defender Gold Portfolio 1983-1994
Land Rover Discovery 1989-1994
Land Rover Story Part One 1948-1971
Fifty Years of Selling Land Rover
Lincoln Gold Portfolio 1949-1960
Lincoln Continental 1961-1969
Lincoln Continental 1969-1976
Lotus Sports Racers Gold Portfolio 1953-1965
Lotus Seven Gold Portfolio 1957-1973
Lotus Caterham Seven Gold Portfolio 1974-1995
Lotus Elan Gold Portfolio 1962-1974
Lotus Elan Collection No. 2 1963-1972
Lotus Elan & SE 1989-1992
Lotus Europa Gold Portfolio 1966-1975
Lotus Elite & Eclat 1974-1982
Lotus Turbo Esprit 1980-1986
Marcos Coupés & Spyders Gold Portfolio 1960-1997
Maserati 1965-1970
Matra Limited Edition 1965-1983
Mazda Miata MX-5 Performance Portfolio 1989-1996
Mazda RX-7 Gold Portfolio 1978-1991
McLaren F1 Sportscar Limited Edition
Mercedes 190 & 300 SL 1954-1963
Mercedes G-Wagen 1981-1994
Mercedes S & 600 1965-1972
Mercedes S Class 1972-1979
Mercedes 230 • 250 • 280SL Gold Portfolio 1963-1971
Mercedes SLs & SLCs Gold Portfolio 1971-1989
Mercedes SLs Performance Portfolio 1989-1994
Mercury Limited Edition 1947-59
Mercury Comet & Cyclone Limited Edition 1960-1970
Mercury Muscle Cars 1966-1971
Cougar Limited Edition 1967-1973
Messerschmitt Gold Portfolio 1954-1964
MG Gold Portfolio 1929-1939
MG TA & TC Gold Portfolio 1936-1949
MG TD & TF Gold Portfolio 1949-1955
MGA & Twin Cam Gold Portfolio 1955-1962
MG Midget Gold Portfolio 1961-1979
MGB Roadsters 1962-1980
MGB MGC & V8 Gold Portfolio 1962-1980
MGB GT 1965-1980
MGC & MGB GT V8 Limited Edition
MG Y-Type & Magnette ZA/ZB Limited Edition
Mini Gold Portfolio 1959-1969
Mini Gold Portfolio 1969-1980
Mini Gold Portfolio 1981-1997
High Performance Minis Gold Portfolio 1960-1973
Mini Cooper Gold Portfolio 1961-1971
Mini Moke Gold Portfolio 1964-1994
Morgan Three-Wheeler Gold Portfolio 1910-1952
Morgan Plus 4 & Four 4 Gold Portfolio 1936-1967
Morgan Cars Gold Portfolio 1968-1989
Morris Minor Collection No. 1 1948-1980
Shelby Mustang Muscle Portfolio 1965-1970
High Performance Mustang IIs 1974-1978
High Performance Mustangs 1982-1988
Nash & Nash-Healey Limited Edition 1949-1957
Nash-Austin Metropolitan Gold Portfolio 1954-1962
Oldsmobile Automobiles 1955-1963
Oldsmobile Muscle Portfolio 1964-1971
Cutlass & 4-4-2 Muscle Portfolio 1964-1974
Oldsmobile Toronado 1966-1978
Opel GT Gold Portfolio 1968-1973
Opel Manta Limited Edition 1970-1975
Packard Gold Portfolio 1946-1958
Pantera Gold Portfolio 1970-1989
Panther Gold Portfolio 1972-1990
Barracuda Muscle Portfolio 1964-1974
Pontiac Tempest & GTO 1961-1965
GTO Muscle Portfolio 1964-1974
Firebird & Trans-Am Muscle Portfolio 1967-1972
Firebird & Trans-Am Muscle Portfolio 1973-1981
High Performance Firebirds 1982-1988
Pontiac Limited Edition 1949-60
Pontiac Fiero 1984-1988
Porsche 356 Gold Portfolio 1953-1965
Porsche 912 Limited Edition
Porsche 911 1965-1969
Porsche 911 1970-1972
Porsche 911 1973-1977
Porsche 911 SC & Turbo Gold Portfolio 1978-1983
Porsche 911 Carrera & Turbo Gold Port. 1984-1989
Porsche 911 Gold Portfolio 1990-1997
Porsche 924 Gold Portfolio 1975-1988
Porsche 928 Performance Portfolio 1977-1994
Porsche 944 Gold Portfolio 1981-1991
Porsche 968 Limited Edition
Range Rover Gold Portfolio 1970-1985
Range Rover Gold Portfolio 1986-1995
Reliant Scimitar 1964-1986
Renault Alpine Gold Portfolio 1958-1994
Riley Gold Portfolio 1924-1939
R.R. Silver Cloud & Bentley 'S' Series Gold P. 1955-1965
Rolls Royce Silver Shadow Gold Portfolio 1965-1980
Rolls Royce & Bentley Gold Portfolio 1980-1989
Rolls Royce & Bentley Limited Edition 1990-1997
Rover P4 1949-1959
Rover 3 & 3.5 Litre Gold Portfolio 1958-1973
Rover 2000 & 2200 1963-1977
Rover 3500 & Vitesse 1976-1986
Saab Sonett Collection No.1 1966-1974
Saab Turbo 1976-1983
Studebaker Gold Portfolio 1947-1966
Studebaker Hawks & Larks 1956-1963
Suzuki SJ Gold Portfolio 1971-1997
Vitara, Sidekick & Geo Tracker Perf. Port. 1988-1997
Avanti 1962-1990
Sunbeam Tiger & Alpine Gold Portfolio 1959-1967
Toyota Land Cruiser Gold Portfolio 1956-1987
Toyota Land Cruiser 1988-1997
Toyota MR2 Gold Portfolio 1984-1997
Triumph Dolomite Sprint Limited Edition
Triumph TR2 & TR3 Gold Portfolio 1952-1961
Triumph TR4, TR5, TR250 1961-1968
Triumph TR6 Gold Portfolio 1969-1976
Triumph TR7 & TR8 Gold Portfolio 1975-1982
Triumph Herald 1959-1971
Triumph Vitesse 1962-1971
Triumph Spitfire Gold Portfolio 1962-1980
Triumph 2000, 2.5, 2500 1963-1977
Triumph GT6 Gold Portfolio 1966-1974
Triumph Stag Gold Portfolio 1970-1977
TVR Gold Portfolio 1959-1986
TVR Performance Portfolio 1986-1994
VW Beetle Gold Portfolio 1935-1967
VW Beetle Gold Portfolio 1968-1991
VW Beetle Collection No.1 1970-1982
VW Karmann Ghia 1955-1982
VW Bus, Camper, Van 1954-1967
VW Bus, Camper, Van 1968-1979
VW Bus, Camper, Van 1979-1989
VW Scirocco 1974-1981
VW Golf GTI 1976-1986
Volvo PV444 & PV544 1945-1965
Volvo Amazon-120 Gold Portfolio 1956-1970
Volvo 1800 Gold Portfolio 1960-1973
Volvo 140 & 160 Series Gold Portfolio 1966-1975
Forty Years of Selling Volvo
Westfield Limited Edition

BROOKLANDS *Road & Track* SERIES

Road & Track on Alfa Romeo 1964-1970
Road & Track on Alfa Romeo 1971-1976
Road & Track on Alfa Romeo 1977-1989
Road & Track on Aston Martin 1962-1990
R & T on Auburn Cord and Duesenburg 1952-84
Road & Track on Audi & Auto Union 1952-1980
Road & Track on Audi & Auto Union 1980-1986
Road & Track on Austin Healey 1953-1970
Road & Track on BMW Cars 1966-1974
Road & Track on BMW Cars 1975-1978
Road & Track on BMW Cars 1979-1983
R & T on Cobra, Shelby & Ford GT40 1962-1992
Road & Track on Corvette 1953-1967
Road & Track on Corvette 1968-1982
Road & Track on Corvette 1982-1986
Road & Track on Corvette 1986-1990
Road & Track on Ferrari 1975-1981
Road & Track on Ferrari 1981-1984
Road & Track on Ferrari 1984-1988
Road & Track on Fiat Sports Cars 1968-1987
Road & Track on Jaguar 1950-1960
Road & Track on Jaguar 1961-1968
Road & Track on Jaguar 1968-1974
Road & Track on Jaguar 1974-1982
Road & Track on Jaguar 1983-1989
Road & Track on Lamborghini 1964-1985
Road & Track on Lotus 1972-1983
R & T on Mazda RX-7 & MX-5 Miata 1986-1991
Road & Track on Mercedes 1952-1962
Road & Track on Mercedes 1963-1970
Road & Track on Mercedes 1971-1979
Road & Track on Mercedes 1980-1987
Road & Track on MG Sports Cars 1949-1961
Road & Track on MG Sports Cars 1962-1980
R & T on Nissan 300-ZX & Turbo 1984-1989
Road & Track on Pontiac 1960-1983
Road & Track on Porsche 1951-1967
Road & Track on Porsche 1968-1971
Road & Track on Porsche 1972-1975
Road & Track on Porsche 1975-1978
Road & Track on Porsche 1979-1982
Road & Track on Porsche 1985-1988
R & T on Rolls Royce & Bentley 1950-1965
R & T on Rolls Royce & Bentley 1966-1984
Road & Track on Saab 1972-1992
R & T on Toyota Sports & GT Cars 1966-1984
R & T on Triumph Sports Cars 1953-1967
R & T on Triumph Sports Cars 1967-1974
R & T on Triumph Sports Cars 1974-1982
Road & Track on Volkswagen 1951-1968
Road & Track on Volkswagen 1968-1978
Road & Track on Volkswagen 1978-1985
Road & Track on Volvo 1957-1974
Road & Track on Volvo 1977-1994
R & T - Henry Manney at Large & Abroad
R & T - Peter Egan's "Side Glances"
R & T - Peter Egan "At Large"

BROOKLANDS *Car and Driver* SERIES

Car and Driver on BMW 1955-1977
Car and Driver on Corvette 1978-1982
Car and Driver on Corvette 1983-1988
C and D on Datsun Z 1600 & 2000 1966-1984
Car and Driver on Ferrari 1955-1962
Car and Driver on Ferrari 1963-1975
Car and Driver on Ferrari 1976-1983
Car and Driver on Mopar 1956-1967
Car and Driver on Mopar 1968-1975
Car and Driver on Mustang 1964-1972
Car and Driver on Pontiac 1961-1975
Car and Driver on Porsche 1955-1962
Car and Driver on Porsche 1963-1970
Car and Driver on Porsche 1970-1976
Car and Driver on Porsche 1977-1981
Car and Driver on Porsche 1982-1986
Car and Driver on Volvo 1955-1986

RACING

Le Mans - The Bentley & Alfa Years - 1923-1939
Le Mans - The Jaguar Years - 1949-1957
Le Mans - The Ferrari Years - 1958-1965
Le Mans - The Ford & Matra Years - 1966-1974
Le Mans - The Porsche Years - 1975-1982
Mille Miglia - The Alfa & Ferrari Years - 1927-1951
Mille Miglia - The Ferrari & Mercedes Years - 1952-57

A COMPREHENSIVE GUIDE

BMW 2002

BROOKLANDS *Practical Classics* SERIES

PC on Austin A40 Restoration
PC on Land Rover Restoration
PC on Metalworking in Restoration
PC on Midget/Sprite Restoration
PC on MGB Restoration
PC on Sunbeam Rapier Restoration
PC on Triumph Herald/Vitesse
PC on Spitfire Restoration

BROOKLANDS *Hot Rod* 'MUSCLECAR & HI-PO ENGINES' SERIES

Chevy 265 & 283
Chevy 302 & 327
Chevy 348 & 409
Chevy 350 & 400
Chevy 396 & 427
Chevy 454 thru 512
Chrysler Hemi
Chrysler 273, 318, 340 & 360
Chrysler 361, 383, 400, 413, 426, 440
Ford 289, 302, Boss 302 & 351W
Ford 351C & Boss 351
Ford Big Block

BROOKLANDS RESTORATION SERIES

Auto Restoration Tips & Techniques
Basic Bodywork Tips & Techniques
BMW 2002 Restoration Guide
Classic Camaro Restoration
Chevrolet High Performance Tips & Techniques
Chevy Engine Swapping Tips & Techniques
Chevy-GMC Pickup Repair
Chrysler Engine Swapping Tips & Techniques
Engine Swapping Tips & Techniques
Ford Pickup Repair
Land Rover Restoration Tips & Techniques
MG 'T' Series Restoration Guide
MGA Restoration Guide
Mustang Restoration Tips & Techniques

MOTORCYCLING

BROOKLANDS ROAD TEST SERIES

AJS & Matchless Gold Portfolio 1945-1966
BMW Motorcycles Gold Portfolio 1950-1971
BMW Motorcycles Gold Portfolio 1971-1976
BSA Singles Gold Portfolio 1945-1963
BSA Singles Gold Portfolio 1964-1974
BSA Twins A7 & A10 Gold Portfolio 1946-1962
BSA Twins A50 & A65 Gold Portfolio 1962-1973
BSA & Triumph Triples Gold Portfolio 1968-1976
Ducati Gold Portfolio 1960-1973
Ducati Gold Portfolio 1974-1978
Ducati Gold Portfolio 1978-1982
Honda CB750 Gold Portfolio 1969-1978
Laverda Gold Portfolio 1967-1977
Moto Guzzi Gold Portfolio 1949-1973
Norton Commando Gold Portfolio 1968-1977
Triumph Bonneville Gold Portfolio 1959-1983
Vincent Gold Portfolio 1945-1980

BROOKLANDS *Cycle World* SERIES

Cycle World on BMW 1974-1980
Cycle World on BMW 1981-1986
Cycle World on Ducati 1982-1991
Cycle World on Harley-Davidson 1962-1968
Cycle World on Harley-Davidson 1978-1983
Cycle World on Harley-Davidson 1983-1987
Cycle World on Harley-Davidson 1987-1990
Cycle World on Harley-Davidson 1990-1992
Cycle World on Honda 1962-1967
Cycle World on Honda 1968-1971
Cycle World on Honda 1971-1974
Cycle World on Husqvarna 1966-1976
Cycle World on Husqvarna 1977-1984
Cycle World on Kawasaki 1966-1971
Cycle World on Kawasaki Off-Road Bikes 1972-1979
Cycle World on Kawasaki Street Bikes 1972-1976
Cycle World on Norton 1962-1971
Cycle World on Suzuki 1962-1970
Cycle World on Suzuki Off-Road Bikes 1971-1976
Cycle World on Suzuki Street Bikes 1971-1976
Cycle World on Triumph 1967-1972
Cycle World on Yamaha 1962-1969
Cycle World on Yamaha Off-Road Bikes 1970-1974
Cycle World on Yamaha Street Bikes 1970-1974

MILITARY

BROOKLANDS MILITARY VEHICLES SERIES

Allied Military Vehicles No.2 1941-1946
Complete WW2 Military Jeep Manual
Dodge Military Vehicles No.1 1940-1945
Hail To The Jeep
Military & Civilian Amphibians 1940-1990
Off Road Jeeps: Civilian & Military 1944-1971
US Military Vehicles 1941-1945
US Army Military Vehicles WW2-TM9-2800
VW Kubelwagen Military Portfolio 1940-1990
WW2 Jeep Military Portfolio 1941-1945

15058

CONTENTS

Page	Title	Publication	Date		Year
5	Chrysler's Aluminum V-10 - The Heart of the Viper	Motor Trend	Sept		1990
6	Snakes Alive!	Car	Sept		1990
12	Cobra vs. Viper Comparison Test	Road & Track Specials	June		1991
20	Viper RT/10	Motor Trend	Nov		1991
28	Dodge Viper	Car South Africa	Jan		1992
32	Viper RT/10 Road Test	Road & Track Specials	Mar		1992
38	Dodge Viper RT/10 Road Test	Motor Trend	Aug		1992
44	Chrysler's Second Coming	Autocar	Aug	26	1992
47	Dodge Viper	Car and Driver Buyer's Guide			1992
48	Dodge Viper RT/10 Road Test	Car and Driver	Mar		1992
52	Stars 'N' Stripes Viper GTS Coupe	Motor Australia	Aug		1993
55	Viper vs. Corvette ZR-1	Car and Driver	Mar		1992
56	Second Strike	Automobile Magazine	Mar		1993
62	Mean Streak	Autocar	Mar	24	1993
66	Hennessey Venom 500 Viper Road Test	Sports Car International	Dec		1993
71	Dodge Viper RT/10	Road & Track Specials			1993
72	Suddenly, it's 1963	Road & Track Specials			1993
80	Mad as a Snake - Hennessey Motorsports Venom 500 Viper	Performance Car	July		1994
83	Viper RT/10 Road Test	Road & Track Specials	May		1994
88	Coupe de Pace	American Car World	July		1994
92	The Supercar Olympics Comparison Test	Car and Driver	July		1995
100	Dodge Viper RT/10 Road Test	Road & Track	Nov		1995
105	Dodge Viper RT/10 Road Test	Car and Driver	Dec		1995
109	Dodge Viper GTS	Road & Track	May		1996
110	Dodge Viper GTS-R	Car and Driver	Apr		1996
114	Reality Check	Automobile Magazine	Apr		1996
122	Dodge Viper GTS	Road & Track Specials			1997
128	Warming the Snake's Blood	Autocar	Jan	1	1997
132	Hennessey Venom 600 GTS Road Test	Motor Trend	Dec		1997
139	Dodge Viper GTS	Car	Feb		1998
140	Dodge Viper GTS & RT/10	Road & Track Specials			1998

ACKNOWLEDGEMENTS

Our first book on the dynamic Vipers recently went out of print and so we have taken the opportunity to completely update it, enlarge it and issue it as one of our Performance Portfolio series and we have in fact kept only the best 25 pages from the earlier book.

Our Performance Portfolio series is dedicated to cars which have either become collectible or are destined to become classics and there is no doubt that the Viper which has already become a legend in its short life will go on to become both collectible and a classic.

Brooklands Books are an archive series for motoring enthusiasts, gathering together in convenient form existing material about interesting cars. They depend for their existence on the generosity and understanding of those who hold the copyright to the material they contain, and we are always pleased to acknowledge the assistance we receive in putting them together. On this occasion our thanks go to the publishers of *American Car World, Autocar, Automobile Magazine, Car, Car and Driver, Car and Driver Buyer's Guide, Car South Africa, Motor Australia, Motor Trend, Performance Car, Road & Track, Road & Track Specials* and *Sports Car International*.

To those people who thought legislation and high insurance premiums had killed the 'muscle car' in the early 1970's, Dodge's startling Viper came as a revelation in the early 1990s. Indeed, for the Viper's designers to get such a car past the bean-counters at Chrysler Corporation was no insignificant feat, and few people who saw the original concept car can have seriously believed that it would some day become a production reality.

R.M. Clarke

This book contains a report comparing the Viper with the legendary AC Cobra - and not without reason. The two-seater Viper was designed as a "back-to-basics" model which would evoke all the raw excitement associated with cars like the Cobra. Yet the Viper is no mere retro-car; it incorporates all the technological advances which were available to its designers in the early 1990s, and it is all the better for that.

The Viper's all-aluminium eight-litre V10 engine was developed with technical assistance from Chrysler-owned Lamborghini, and it puts out 450bhp with a staggering 490/lb/ft of torque in GTS form. Driving through a six-speed manual transmission, it powers the Viper to 60 mph in 4.4 seconds and then on to a top speed of 180mph. And its modern technology means that the Viper does not suffer from the poor brakes and handling so often associated with the great muscle cars of the 1960's. Not only does it handle superbly, but according to factory figures it can accelerate from a standstill to 100mph and then be safely braked back to zero, in less than 14.5 seconds.

For those fortunate enough to own a Viper, and for those who can only dream, this book will be a welcome companion.

James Taylor

CHRYSLER'S ALUMINUM V-10

THE HEART OF THE VIPER
by Don Sherman

Shortly after the Dodge Viper design study appeared on the auto-show circuit in January 1989, more than a few premature deposit checks were mailed to Chrysler's Highland Park, Michigan, head office. As it turns out, customers were *not* stirred to a check-writing frenzy solely by the Viper's sensuous open-roadster curves. Raw sports-car sex appeal has been readily available in America for years. Rather, the Viper's unique feature and the prime attraction to those eager for a place on the production-car waiting list is a thumping 8-liter V-10 under the muscular hood.

The idea of powering the Viper with such an extraordinary engine had an appropriately unusual origin. Several years ago, Dodge Ram pickup trucks fell into a sales slump. The Chrysler team dispatched to analyze the problem discovered that the Ram's most powerful 5.9-liter V-8 engine wasn't potent enough to fulfill certain customer needs. Chevy and Ford pickups both offered big-block V-8s with more than seven liters of piston displacement to tow extra-heavy loads, such as horse haulers and travel trailers.

Unfortunately, there was no easy way for Chrysler to add muscle to its Ram pickup truck. The tooling that once produced the corporation's big-block V-8s had long ago been scrapped and the 5.9-liter small block could not be stretched far enough by conventional means to match the torque curves available in Chevy and Ford pickups.

To save the day, Chrysler President Bob Lutz concocted a bold but wacky solution: Why not simply tack on an extra pair of cylinders onto the 5.9-liter V-8 to create a strapping V-10 that could be manufactured on existing tooling? The naysayers promptly stormed out of the woodwork. Technical foes insisted that a 90° V-10 engine would be horribly out of balance; shaking forces would be unbearable, even in a truck, they claimed. Marketing opponents declared the idea too radically different from the conventional Chevrolet and Ford approach and that the truck-buying public would never accept such an oddball engine design.

Lutz, however, persisted. He pointed out that 5-cylinder engines by Audi and Mercedes-Benz were perfectly acceptable, that the V-10 was an established truck engine configuration in both Europe and Japan. Eventually, he gained one ally, then more. An experimental V-10 engine was created by literally brazing together portions of the existing V-8's castings. When it was first fired up on the dynamometer, it ran more smoothly than expected. There were no serious vibration problems. Lutz and his supporters were vindicated.

There are several reasons why no auto manufacturer has recently adopted a V-10 layout. Such engines are inevitably heavy and bulky. For optimum vibration characteristics, the proper angle between cylinder banks is 72°, another strike against Chrysler's approach. In spite of these drawbacks, this layout may be gaining in popularity. Honda, Renault, Judd, and Alfa Romeo have all designed V-10s for Formula One racing, and the all-new '91 Acura Legend Coupe may be powered by such an engine when it debuts this fall.

Chrysler's V-10 configuration for the Viper and future Dodge truck engines is not ideal, but there appears nothing to keep it from doing a remarkable job pulling horses and producing horsepower. Essentially, this is an all-new design that retains the 5.9-liter V-8's bore centers and deck heights. Since the cylinder-bank angle is 90° instead of the theoretically correct 72°, there's an uneven firing pattern. The interval between power pulses alternates between 54 and 90° of crankshaft rotation. Primary forces are in balance, but a secondary lateral shake exists, which, according to a Chrysler engineer, is smaller in magnitude than the typical V-6 disturbance.

The Chrysler V-10's cylinder block has a number of heavy-duty features in keeping with its intended application: free-standing cast iron cylinder liners, ladder-type main-bearing girdle, and deep side skirts with a wavy surface to minimize radiated noise. The cylinder heads have an advanced high-efficiency combustion chamber and a conventional pushrod valvetrain in keeping with the Viper's "retrotech" image. Nevertheless, a great deal of contemporary technology is incorporated in the V-10's design: distributorless ignition, roller-type hydraulic valve lifters, tuned intake and exhaust plumbing, sequential port fuel injection, computerized engine management, single-belt accessory drive, and aluminum castings for all major components. (While Lamborghini assisted in the conversion of the design to aluminum, production castings will be sourced in the U.S. Truck versions of the engine—not due for several years—will most likely use a cast iron block and heads.)

With a 4.00-in. bore and a 3.88-in. stroke, the Viper's virile heart displaces a full 8 liters (488 cu in.). Merle Liskey, executive engineer in Chrysler's Jeep Truck Engineering department, asserts that there will be no problem meeting the Viper's conservative output projections: 400 hp and 450 lb-ft of torque.

Vibration created by the uneven firing order is clearly not a problem. Liskey claims the aluminum V-10 weighs about the same as an iron V-8. The exhaust note sounds more serpentine than spirited, but the Viper hasn't yet undergone voice training. That procedure may not be necessary: When the accelerator is mashed, the howl of protest by the rear pair of Goodyear Eagle GTs will doubtlessly drown out all lesser sounds.

SNAKES ALIVE!

Chrysler's mind-blowing 8.0 litre Viper is the Cobras successor for the '90s. Georg Kacher tries it

PHOTOGRAPHS BY MARK PRESTON

DODGE VIPER

WE CAN HEAR THE VIPER long before it snakes into sight. Its engine howls and gurgles as project engineer Neil Hannemann manoeuvres the car inside the cordoned-off prototype shop. Engulfed by V10 thunder, even the hard-boiled proving-ground veterans prick up their ears, relishing every stab of the throttle.

The raucous red roadster is living proof that Chrysler is driving towards a brighter future. At the gate where the beast rolls out of the shadow and into the bright afternoon sun, the workers greet it by raising their caps and making Churchillian victory gestures.

The Viper, source of all this excitement, is no mere show car: Chrysler chairman Lee Iacocca announced in May that the first production cars will be ready in January 1992, less than four years after the project was first mooted.

The Viper was born on 28 May, 1988. On that day, the Chrysler management decided to prepare a two-seater sports car for the 1989 Detroit Auto Show. The public response to the striking roadster was so enthusiastic that Highland Park had no choice but to examine the feasibility of putting it into low-volume production.

To carry out this task, 'Team Viper' was formed. It consists of about 50 volunteers from the engineering, design, manufacturing and purchasing staff who work together (and with the suppliers) as if the team were a separate company. In the 12 months that followed, Team Viper – headed by Roy Sjoberg – convinced the Chrysler management that the drop-top eye-catcher has got what it takes.

Senior designer Tom Gale's proposal was accepted pretty much unchanged. The round auxiliary driving lamps in the front bumper disappeared, the side pipes were concealed for reasons of safety and rigidity, the windscreen was altered to meet various legal requirements, and the rear apron was lowered slightly to reduce axle lift.

But there was no reason to touch the basic shape, which looks muscular, aggressive and as uncompromising as a 21st-century Cobra. The Viper is wide, long and low, but it's certainly no masterpiece of space utilisation. The boot is small, and the cabin is a leather-lined cocoon for two – sorry, no hand luggage, please. This really is a nice-weather car, but if you insist, Chrysler will fit a token convertible top with curtain side windows and zero theft protection.

Unlike the body, the underpinnings have changed quite a bit since the car first

> **'Engulfed by V10 thunder, even the hard-boiled proving-ground veterans prick up their ears, relishing every stab of the Viper's throttle'**

rolled into the limelight. Neil Hannemann, who worked for Carroll Shelby before joining Team Viper, explains: 'To keep the car inexpensive and simple, we originally planned to fit a truck engine, and the suspension of a pick-up. But the first chassis mule, completed in August 1989, showed quite clearly that this common-components concept wasn't good enough for such a high-visibility vehicle. So, instead of sticking to the sport-utility hardware, we developed a proper double wishbone suspension. The only carry-over

Test Viper's interior provisional. Production car will have a parking brake, revised instrument panel

items that will make it into the production car are the upper A-arms of the front suspension, which stem from our pick-up.'

With the clamshell bonnet taken off (it will be properly front-hinged on the next prototype), the car's mechanicals are displayed as if on a tray. The Viper follows the Lotus philosophy of relying on a steel backbone chassis using steel outriggers and steel subframes to accommodate the suspension elements and the engine.

The massive springs and the gas-pressure shock absorbers are mounted at a negative angle, the anti-roll bars are unusually fat and adjustable, and through all the pitch-black metal you can catch an occasional glimpse of the massive – 14-inch – vented brake discs.

Prototype number two – pictured here – was equipped with experimental wheels made by Boyds. But the final production version will boast one-piece cast-aluminium wheels shod with 335/35ZR17 rubber in the back and with 275/40ZR17 tyres in the front. Team Viper has yet to decide whether to use the Eagle ZRs fitted to our photographic car, or a special compound that would be supplied by the same manufacturer.

Simplicity was obviously high on the priority list compiled by the engineers and designers. That's why the Viper does without adjustable dampers, traction control, air-conditioning, 4wd, 4ws and anti-lock braking.

No ABS? 'Not at the moment,' says chief engineer François Castaing. 'This is a controversial issue. There are those who maintain that the Viper does not need ABS, just as a Formula One racer does not need ABS. But, of course, we know that not all customers out there are Ayrton Sennas, so we've made provision for fitting anti-lock brakes at a later stage.'

Castaing reckons Chrysler will build 400 Vipers a year at first, rising to 5000. The series-1 model is the car you see on these pages, but the series-2 might have a modified body, and the series-3 will probably use a V8 engine and ABS brakes.

The majestic 8.0-litre pushrod V10 that sits between the front

8.0-litre V10-powered Viper will do 160mph, and 0-100mph in under 10 seconds, all with a raucous roar

wheels, started life as a humble truck engine. But the old iron block was 175lb heavier than the new aluminium unit, and it was a touch too rough and uncultivated for a serious sports car. This is why Chrysler approached Lamborghini for help. Lamborghini's technical director Mauro Forghieri himself looked after the project. The engine was given a light-alloy block, modified valves and ports, and countless detail improvements.

The basic two-valve layout, however, remained unchanged: 'There was really no need to switch to four valves per cylinder,' says Hannemann. 'On the contrary: a 32-valve head produces so much power that we would have been forced to reduce the displacement. But we're not looking for maximum bhp numbers, we're looking for maximum low-end torque. And that's what the two-valve V10 is all about.'

The 488cu in (that's almost 8.0 litres) powerplant is expected to develop 400bhp at 5000rpm and 450lb ft at 2400rpm. We say expected, because the first aluminium engine is about to be bench-tested as we go to press. The iron-block V10 fitted to the test car is redlined at 5500rpm, but the lightweight unit should be able to spin to 6000rpm.

The Chrysler people are a little evasive about the performance figures because they don't know yet whether the Viper can be trimmed to meet its target weight of 3000lb. If it does, the car will be able to accelerate in 'under five seconds' from 0-60mph. The exact figure the engineers have in mind is '3.999 seconds, but we'll be almost as happy when she does it in 4.2 or 4.3 seconds'. The roadster will storm from 0-100mph in under 10 seconds, and it can reach a maximum speed of about 160mph. If Chrysler were to spend an extra $2000 on tyres, it could even top 180mph, apparently.

With a car like this, the project engineers are much more interested in talking about performance than fuel economy. Since the first prototypes seldom bettered 8mpg when driven hard and 14mpg when driven less ambitiously, the petrol tank capacity is currently under revision: 'The Viper is not

Styling is muscular, aggressive. A convertible top is available, but really Viper is a fair-weather car

exactly light on fuel,' admits François Castaing, 'but because this car won't be built in large numbers it won't hurt our CAFE fuel economy rating too much.'

Climbing behind the leather-rimmed three-spoke steering wheel is no joke: you have to reach for the inside door handle – there's no exterior handle, and there are no door locks, either. The sills are tall and wide, but

9

Cockpit is cramped, but the adjustable, leather-trimmed, duo-tone seats are surprisingly good

the leather-trimmed seats are surprisingly comfortable, and generously adjustable. Even when you're 6ft 8in tall, driving the Dodge Viper is the easiest trick in the book.

The interior is plain and tasteful, but the instrument panel in our mule is strictly provisional; the real dashboard will look more like that of the show car. The dominant shades are grey and black, but the duotone seats reflect the colour of the body, which is available in a choice of red, white or black.

So provisional is the interior, that it doesn't even have a parking brake yet, and the dials and warning lights have not been finalised. At the moment, the facia is dominated by the speedo and rev-counter, which are flanked by four smaller instruments depicting water and oil temperature, oil pressure and battery voltage. The so-called superlight headlamps – a late tribute to the Dodge Polara 500 – are activated by a simple pull-button.

The generic heater and ventilation controls are within easy reach of driver and passenger, and air-conditioning will be a dealer-installed option – the sound system is one of the very few factory-fitted extras. The series-1 cars will be available only with the six-speed Getrag manual transmission, but at a later stage, Chrysler may offer a four-speed automatic option.

The five-point racing harness will eventually give way to a conventional inertia-reel belt. The pedals, which are slightly

Viper has no exterior door handles or locks, so you must reach inside to gain access. Climbing in not easy

offset, will be repositioned, and the lower half of the dashboard will be cut out to provide a little more kneeroom.

Time to hit the road. The engine fires at the first turn of the key and quickly settles to a rock-solid idle at about 700rpm.

Test Viper's bonnet can be removed to display mechanicals. On the next prototype, it will be front-hinged

DODGE VIPER

> 'This crowd-stopping two-seater roadster is definitely the most exciting car that has come out of Detroit for a long, long time'

Unlike most supercar engines, the V10 is no prima donna. Throttle response is progressive but not sensationally fast, and the engine doesn't rev as willingly as it might.

Its running characteristics are shirt-sleeved, and not all that well mannered, but when you stab the throttle to release an avalanche of torque, the Viper bares its fangs and teaches the big names a lesson they won't forget in a hurry.

The great feature of this car is that you don't need advanced driving lessons to get the best out of it. Take the engine, for instance – it's not a highly tuned bag of nerves, but an obedient torque generator. The clutch isn't a do-it-or-stall-it guillotine, but a well balanced and perfectly progressive master of the power flood-gate. And the transmission isn't a set of undersynchronised hostile cogs but slick, quick and light.

Fourth and sixth are a little close together, but according to Hannemann that's just a matter of fine-tuning the linkage. Whether the Viper actually needs six gears is debatable. After all, fifth and sixth are both designed as rev-cutting overdrive ratios: 4500rpm in fifth corresponds to 140mph, 1500rpm in sixth equals 60mph.

The clutch and accelerator may be ideally weighted, but the brake pedal is definitely on the heavy side. This will be changed by giving the existing brakes more vacuum assistance, and there's talk of more powerful brakes, especially at the rear. The conventional power-assisted steering is also going to be modified. It is presently too light around the straight-ahead position, and turn-in is a touch too aggressive.

Team Viper is also considering changes to the car's handling. Hannemann explains: 'We're quite happy with the basic set-up. The car is easy to drive and forgiving at the limit. But there's a little too much understeer for the enthusiast driver, and we are going to change that. The roadholding is already exactly where we want it, and the weight distribution will be a perfect 50:50, once the aluminium engine is available.'

Even at relatively moderate engine speeds, the fat Goodyears struggle to translate all that oomph into traction. Since the torque curve is virtually flat between 2000 and 4800rpm, you can leave black rubber marks on the tarmac, in any of the first three gears. In the rain, this car must be quite a handful to drive – but so is the Corvette, and so is the Cobra.

After a brief blast down the straight, we go to the handling course at the back of the track. Through those fast esses, body roll is conspicuously absent and since the car sticks like glue, your brain soon starts playing roller-coaster inside your head. Acceleration and deceleration are equally impressive.

In a car like this you're not looking for exceptional ride comfort, but the way the Viper floats over the pock-marked part of the test track is little short of sensational. While crests and longer undulations are ironed out with incredible ease, pot-holes, ridges and broken-up surfaces shake the car to its very foundation.

Although you can hear and

Viper's 400bhp 8.0-litre pushrod V10 started life as a truck engine. Has since had some modification

feel the composite body panels fighting and groaning under the extreme stress, the second Viper prototype fares no worse than a run-of-the-mill Corvette. But there exists one area where the red thunderball instantly jumps to the top of the league, and that's noise.

The large-diameter tailpipes shout you down above 2500rpm, and from there on, engine, tyre and wind noise will fill your eardrums until they're ready to crack at the seams. Since there are no side windows, you end up putting your arm on the door to divert the hurricane; and since the Viper has no roof, you'd best put on a tight-fitting cap to save your hair.

Despite the streamlined hairstyle and the bongo drums inside my ears, I climbed out of the Viper with a very big smile on my face. This crowd-stopping two-seater is definitely the most exciting car that has come out of Detroit for a long, long time. Of course, it is not perfect, but the simple fact that it jumped all the bureaucratic hurdles with bravado speaks not only for the product, but also for Chrysler's belief in a better tomorrow.

At the moment, Team Viper has yet to answer a few crucial questions. The special task force located in the Jeep truck engineering area must, above all, decide on an assembly site.

The Viper squad is currently also in the process of sourcing key components such as body, chassis and suspension from various outside suppliers. The first vehicles will be shipped to selected Dodge dealers who are going to charge 'under $50,000' (£30,000) – plus premium – for the privilege of owning one of the early Vipers. Initially, the car will be sold only in America, but there is a possibility that the series-2 or 3 may make it across the Atlantic.

'The Viper is more than just a new sports car,' says Francois Castaing. 'For us, it's also a new formula that may have a big future. If it works, the team concept will be transferred to other projects. Why shouldn't there be a whole generation of low-volume, low-investment niche vehicles? Right now, I can't be more specific – but maybe we'll have a little surprise for you at the next Detroit Auto Show in January.

COBRA vs VIPER

SNAKES, RATTLE & ROLL

BY RAY THURSBY
PHOTOS BY LESLIE L. BIRD & DEAN SIRACUSA

Words fail me. Descriptive phrases, neatly turned sentences that make dull cars exciting and exciting cars irresistible, just don't fall readily to mind when it's time to make some sense of the meeting between a 1966 Shelby Cobra and a 1992 Dodge Viper. Call it sensory overload, numbness, that period of tingling nerve ends and jumbled thoughts that inevitably follows a bungee jump, a trip in an F-15 fighter plane or a ride in what may be the most exciting performance machines that ever pounded pavement.

Yes, I know there are cars that can outrun the Super Snakes. I've ridden in—and even driven—a few myself. But that's beside the point. Nails can be driven with the smallest of hammers; a 10-lb sledge makes a bigger impression, even though it's doing the same thing.

Perhaps it is the tightly focused single-purpose nature of these two beasts. Each has an oversize engine, enough pieces to get the engine's power to the ground, a rudimentary body, two seats and a steering wheel for the driver to hang on to. No elaborate radios, no electric windows—hell, no windows at all, unless you want to attach them yourself—and only the most minimal concessions to civility as demanded by bureaucracy.

Despite the differences in number of cylinders under the hood, appearance and specification, these are the same car at heart. Neither bears any resemblance at all to the assembly line products of manufacturers' bread-and-butter teams; they carry the stamp of the individuals who created them.

To a large degree, both cars owe their existence to Carroll Shelby, one of the least timid of men. Don't let the carefully created and well-honed image of a good ol' Texas boy wearing bib overalls deceive you: Shelby is one shrewd

■ **This 427 Cobra sports a rare intake manifold, which accommodates four Weber 52-mm IDA carburetors. Halibrand mags help put more than 400 bhp down to the ground.**

cookie, not averse to earning money or getting publicity for himself and/or his products.

Which financial rewards and publicity, let it be said, have been earned. Shelby is, after all, the one who thought up the Cobra, and got it into production. Before the Cobra era, he was a talented and successful racing driver, afterwards a builder of high-performance Chrysler products, with a few side ventures thrown in for good measure. It wouldn't do to underestimate the man or his accomplishments.

The Cobra story has been told any number of times, has been the subject of exhaustive scrutiny; there isn't much to add at this late date. Shelby saw potential in the marriage of British chassis and American engine, and convinced AC and Ford to play along. Early Cobras, powered by the then-new Ford 289-cu-in. V-8, proved his initial assessment right.

But the early Cobras had their limitations, centered mostly around their transverse-leaf spring suspensions. No real surprise that a chassis setup developed in the early Fifties for use with low-power engines was not quite up to even the 271 bhp of the basic Cobra engine.

Stuffing a 427-cu-in. V-8 into one of those early Cobras, as the late Ken Miles did under Shelby's direction, made matters worse. More speed was available, but making use of it was, to say the least, a tricky proposition. The final production 427 Cobra ended up with a new frame and a completely redesigned suspension. As such, it became a car that mere mortals could drive. If they were careful.

■ The Viper's engine has an additional two pistons and 500 cc over the Cobra's 427-cu-in. mill. Fuel injection allows more power and equal civility.

In the end, the Cobra was a success. It won races, made money for Shelby, got lots of favorable publicity for Ford, and staved off the collapse of AC Cars (which didn't occur until just this past year). Everybody got something out of the deal, not least among them the collectors who ended up with the original cars and the entrepreneurs who built a thriving business selling reproductions.

■

By contrast, the story of the Viper's conception and gestation has yet to be told. It has been said that the idea originated within the Shelby operation and that the concept, if not the first prototype, was transferred to a development group within Chrysler. Early rumors did indeed concern a "new Shelby sports car," and Ol' Shel himself was indeed on hand when the Viper was publicly unveiled. How it *really* happened is a tale that will have to wait for another time.

What is clear, however, is that the Viper was influenced by the Cobra. Its very concept, not to mention its name, represents unabashed homage paid to the ultimate Original Snake of 25 years ago.

Not a bad base on which to build.

Shed of their skins, both snakes can be described thus: A multi-tube structure forms the basic chassis, carrying fully independent suspension. Within that frame, a large iron-block pushrod engine is inserted, driving the rear wheels. Disc brakes are fitted at each corner, and curb weight has been kept below 3000 lb. From there, the two cars' makeups diverge.

Before we go any further, though, please understand that the Viper is a prototype and that many details of its appearance and specification are still being reviewed. It seems certain that Chrysler wouldn't dare put it on the market with a turbo-4 under the hood, but individual items are still subject to change.

Ford developed the 427 (7.0-liter) engine used in the Cobra for performance. Installed in Galaxie sedans of the day, it became a fixture in NASCAR racing, and powered the later Ford GTs that so effectively trounced Ferrari in sports car competition. It was a passenger-car engine massaged to provide the ultimate in horsepower at a time when GM and Chrysler were mounting race track challenges with their own race-worthy V-8s. As provided to Shelby, the 427 developed 425 bhp and churned out 480 lb-ft of torque.

The Viper's engine is not likely to end up under the hood of a family sedan. It is a truck

engine, destined for use in upcoming Dodge utility vehicles. Though 8.0 liters is nothing to sneeze at, what sets this engine apart from other production powerplants is not so much its displacement as its configuration: 10 cylinders, arranged in vee-formation. Henry Ford messed around with prototype V-10s more than 60 years ago, but Dodge's will be the first one available to the public. In current form, the Viper V-10 puts out an estimated 400 bhp and 450 lb-ft of torque. With Lamborghini's help, Dodge is preparing an alloy-block version of the V-10 for production Vipers. Nevertheless, the cast-iron device used in this prototype, while perhaps too heavy and prosaic for the customers, seems appropriate for this story.

Manual transmissions are found in both cars. Cobras were fitted with Ford-built 4-speed gearboxes; the Viper unit has two additional ratios and comes from Getrag. Floor-mounted shifters are the rule here, with the edge going to the Viper's straight lever over the Cobra's curiously bent and somewhat awkward fitting one.

Clothed respectively in aluminum and fiberglass, the Cobra and Viper can easily be told apart with a single glance. The Cobra's body shape was old when the car was new, having been developed from a design that began as a copy of the Touring-body Ferrari 166 Barchetta. As engine and tire sizes grew, it was stretched in every direction to meet new requirements. Small chrome-plated "nerf bars" provided all the bumper protection then thought necessary. It remains a handsome, muscular, classic shape.

The Viper owes its body design largely to some overheated imaginations at Chrysler. From front to rear it sweeps, swoops and swirls around in a manner far too assertive for application to everyday cars. Being lower, wider and longer than the Cobra, the Viper gave its stylists every opportunity to create dramatic visual statements with a minimum of hindrance from reality, which they did. I'm undecided about my impression of it; I *think* I like it, and the Viper will never be lost in a crowd.

■

Interior design of the two machines reflects a sameness of purpose and difference of birthplaces. The Cobra is a British sports car inside, with lots of instruments spread across a flat panel, barely acceptable seating for two, and a wood-rim steering wheel for the driver. Restyle the whole thing, add better seats and replace wood with leather wrapping, and you have the Viper cockpit. Taller occupants won't

SHELBY COBRA 427 PROVIDED BY STEVE BERRES, PHOENIX, ARIZONA

have to go through contortions to fit in the Viper as they must in the Cobra; but they will note that function has not been compromised. Advantage: Dodge (to coin a phrase), with honorable mention to the AC.

Barring the unforeseen, Dodge expects to produce an initial run of less than 500 Vipers for the 1992 model year. Quantities half and double that size have been publicly discussed, because no one really knows the dimensions of the Viper market for sure, but 500 seems a nice round figure. Price? The target number is around $60,000 which, given the enormous investment Chrysler must have in the project, is entirely fair. Granted, the Viper is meant more as an image-enhancer than a profit generator, but the stockholders will no doubt be happier if the project comes close to breaking even. Expect a long line at the Viper order desk.

Déjà vu time: Shelby built fewer than 400 Cobra 427s at a list price of $6995 each. At that, the last few were, some say, a hard sell. How times (and prices and attitudes) have changed!

On to the showdown: Snake vs Snake. If the Viper has a rival, the Cobra is it. None of today's high-tech marvels from overseas can do more than put up numbers against these Leviathans, and numbers mean little. This is a story of elemental performance, sheer ground-shaking power, having nothing at all to do with creature comforts or fuel mileage tests. The faint of heart and weak of limb would be most uncomfortable on this ride.

Ride is the operative word where the Viper is concerned. Civilians have not driven the Viper prototypes to date, but a few rides have been given out to journalists. Mine came with Chrysler honcho Bob Lutz in the left seat. Lutz is no stranger to high-performance machinery, and has had enough time in the Viper to feel at home with it. The evidence gathered this day suggests that drivers of more limited talent should approach the Viper with care.

Key turned, the big V-10 lights off with a rumble that is initially disconcerting to bent-8 fans. Logically, it sounds much like two Audi inline-5s coupled together. But once under way, its bark is remarkable.

So's the bite. We're quickly up to high speed,

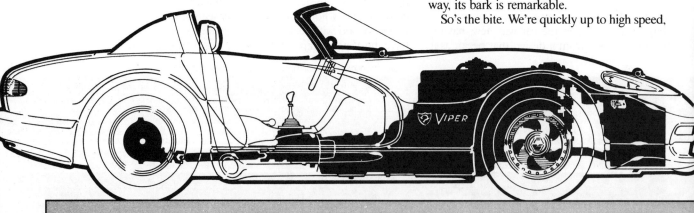

Dodge Viper

SPECIFICATIONS
Price	na
Curb weight	2990 lb
Wheelbase	96.2 in.
Track, f/r	59.6 in./60.8 in.
Length	172.0 in.
Width	75.6 in.
Height	46.2 in.
Fuel capacity	na

CHASSIS & BODY
Layout	front engine/rear drive
Brake system, f/r	discs/discs
Wheels, f/r	alloy, 17-in. diameter
Tires	275/40ZR-17 f, 335/35ZR-17 r
Steering type	rack & pinion
Suspension, f/r	upper & lower A-arms, coil springs, tube shocks, anti-roll bar/multi-link, coil springs, tube shocks, anti-roll bar

ENGINE & DRIVETRAIN
Engine	ohv V-10
Bore x stroke	101.6 x 98.6 mm
Displacement	7989 cc
Compression ratio	na
Horsepower, SAE net	est 400 bhp @ 5500 rpm
Torque	est 450 lb-ft @ 2200 rpm
Fuel injection	electronic port
Transmission	6-sp manual
Final-drive ratio	na

PERFORMANCE
0–60 mph	est 4.1 sec
Standing ¼ mile	est 12.5 sec
Top speed	est 190 mph

na means information is not available.

fast enough to permit use of the Getrag 6-speeder's long top gear. Ride and handling qualities are, as you'd expect, firm and precise, biased toward maximum grip and stability.

It is comfortable in the Viper (and drafty, of course); it looks as wide from inside the cockpit as it does from the outside. The prototype's 5-point seatbelts are much appreciated at 3-digit speeds as is the effectiveness of the four giant disc brakes. Impressive. (As an aside, Lutz confesses to wishing the Feds would allow 5-point seatbelts; it seems, alas, that passive restraint belts are inevitable. Phooey.)

The Cobra is louder than the Viper, just as drafty, feels faster, rides even more harshly and is equally wonderful. The noise from under the hood drowns out, well, everything. There seems to be more feedback through the steering, possibly less ultimate grip in corners, which is logical when you consider the years of technology that have come between Snakes.

Though my Viper experience was confined to long straights and gentle, sweeping bends, I sense in the car the potential for becoming a double handful on twisty roads. I know that is true of the Cobra. There's only the finest of lines—and the slightest change in right foot pressure—between being on the ragged edge and being in way over your head.

Fortunately, this is one of those times when drawing a conclusion is unnecessary. I love the Viper and Cobra, and would cheerfully make room in the garage for either (or both). Under duress, I'd opt for the Original Snake out of pure sentiment, and because of a sneaking hunch that the Cobra, unfettered by the rules and regulations that affect the Viper, might be just a little hairier and faster.

But the Viper is what's coming up next; give the Iacocca and Lutz duo credit for that. There are no more new Cobras, just new Vipers on the way in less than a year.

Give most of the credit to Carroll Shelby, though. Seeing the two machines together, you'd think he never stopped building Cobras, but decided simply to name the latest version after a different snake. ∎

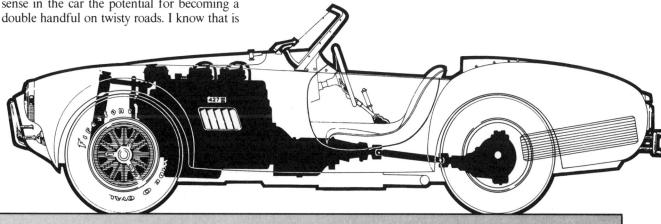

Shelby Cobra

SPECIFICATIONS	
1966 price	$7495
Curb weight	2530 lb
Wheelbase	90.0 in.
Track, f/r	56.0 in./56.0 in.
Length	156.0 in.
Width	68.0 in.
Height	49.0 in.
Fuel capacity	18.0 U.S. gal.

CHASSIS & BODY	
Layout	front engine/rear drive
Brake system, f/r	11.63-in. discs/10.75-in. discs
Wheels, f/r	cast alloy, 15 x 7½-in.
Tires	Goodyear Blue Dot, 8.15 x 15
Steering type	rack & pinion
Suspension, f/r	upper & lower A-arms, coil springs, tube shocks/upper & lower A-arms, coil springs, tube shocks

ENGINE & DRIVETRAIN	
Engine	ohv V-8
Bore x stroke	108.0 x 96.2 mm
Displacement	6998 cc
Compression ratio	11.5:1
Horsepower, SAE gross	425 bhp @ 6000 rpm
Torque	480 lb-ft @ 3700 rpm
Carburetion	2 Holley 4-bbl
Transmission	4-sp manual
Final-drive ratio	3.54:1

PERFORMANCE[1]	
0–60 mph	5.3 sec
Standing ¼ mile	13.8 sec @ 106 mph
Top speed	162 mph

[1] from Cobra 427 road test in *Road & Track*, July 1974.

THE VERY FIRST
VIPER RT/10
DRIVE

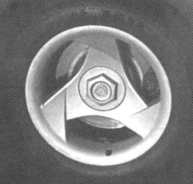

How badly do you want to know about this car?
Badly enough to read about us driving a really awful prototype?

I think the guy wanted me to say, "Wow! God! I can't stand it! Give me more!" I was climbing out of the very first lap turned by a journalist in Dodge's soon-to-be-released supercar—yes, the Viper. (Bells, whistles, twenty-one-gun salute, skyrockets, flags waving, women fainting.)

Engineers, mechanics, the public relations team, a handful of select automotive writers, and a company photographer were clustered around me as I loosened the harness that had belted Carroll Shelby into this very seat as he paced this year's Indianapolis 500. A video camera was rolling.

BY JEAN LINDAMOOD

PHOTOGRAPHY BY GREG JAREM

DODGE VIPER RT/10

I *know* these people were excited about their car. The close-knit, experimental Viper team had been working like dogs for thirty months to put Chrysler president Bob Lutz's 1989 Detroit show car on the road. There was no talking to them unless it was Viper talk. They were consumed with Viper fever. This would be Dodge's Corvette. No, it would be Dodge's *Cobra*. With Carroll Shelby in the thick of things as agitator, father figure, walking encyclopedia, and pace-car driver, the Viper could only be billed as the Cobra of the Nineties. It was the badass Cobra image the Viper team was after as its people crammed as much engine as possible under the hood (an 8.0-liter, 400-bhp V-10), as little creature comfort as they could get away with in the cabin, and the hugest whack of torque (450 pounds-feet) they could dial in without flipping the 3272-pound Viper on its head with the first stomp on the accelerator.

You have been reading stories about the Viper for the past two years. You already know how the "car guys" within the bowels of the corporation were sought out, identified, and courted to form the elite eighty-five-person Viper team headed up by Roy Sjoberg, who defected from General Motors in 1985.

The fourth guy to sign up, vehicle

It was the badass Cobra image the Viper team was after as its people crammed as much engine as possible under the hood.

synthesis manager Herb Helbig, talks about his recruitment: "I heard there was a chance that they might do this car for production. Initially, I wasn't interested in working on it. From an engineering standpoint, from a car guy's view, here was an opportunity of a lifetime. But I enjoyed my job, and I didn't want to take the risk of going off on some boondoggle, having it blow up in my face, and not having the opportunity to come back to my job. But this car had a patron saint who carried some weight, and that was Bob Lutz. I thought, as long as the patron saint doesn't change, this thing's got a prayer."

You have read about iconoclastic president Bob Lutz [September 1991], about his prodigious driving ability and enthusiast sensibilities. About the five-minute conversation he had with engineering vice-president François Castaing and design vice-president Tom Gale that set this project in motion.

You've read about Bob Lutz's plan to show the world that a clean-sheet car can be produced in Detroit in a mere thirty-six months. "It's more like a thirty-month program," says Helbig. "By the time we got the team put together and went through the feasibility phase, we were six months down the road."

You have read how the engine was

Q&A

ROBERT A. LUTZ

President, Chrysler Corporation

When did you decide that the Viper had to see production?
It became glaringly obvious when we started getting a flood of letters. When the mail runs that heavily from people saying, "This is the car of my dreams. This is what I've always wanted. I was too young for the Cobra, I didn't have enough money, I'm not going to let this one get away from me," it's a drumbeat. You read magazine and newspaper articles urging you to build it. It became apparent so quickly that, shortly after the Detroit show, we started organizing a team around [executive engineer] Roy Sjoberg.

Did Lee Iacocca take a lot of coaxing?
Lee was very much in favor of the project. He said that it's in difficult times that you have to do stuff like this to generate excitement both inside and outside the company. And he could see the benefits of taking the team approach to its limit and learning how to do things faster. He has been a very strong supporter.

It's a radical departure for Chrysler.
It's important for us to break the myth that all we know how to do is variations of the K-car platform. The Viper will reestablish our reputation for engineering excellence and help reestablish some sort of faith in America's ability to respond quickly. I think it may be the first manifestation in all of Detroit that the Japanese are not the only ones who can figure trick ways of putting people on wheels. And here's Chrysler, one of the dumb old Detroit Big Three, clearly with people who can think up exciting new concepts, and who aren't stuck endlessly repeating things we've done before.

How do you answer people who say this car is morally irresponsible?
I would say it's not. This is going to be a car that people have as a source of pleasure, much like people have horses, light aircraft, or boats. It's no more necessary for the earth as a source of transportation than a forty-foot cabin cruiser is. It probably will result in a degree of fuel consumption that otherwise wouldn't be necessary, but so many of the alternatives would have a similar effect. We've made the car safe. It's going to be an extremely clean engine. And its fuel economy is certainly better than that of other exotic cars of its type.

Is the Viper ready for Europe?
It's ready, and our distributors over there are clamoring for it. In fact, they want pre-production and pilot versions that have no VIN and can't be registered in the States. They're saying, "Send them over, and we'll figure out a way to get them off the boat."

This car is pretty basic. Do you think people will be expecting too much?
If we have any worry at all, it's that we may be wearing out our welcome with the enthusiast press. We don't want you all to think you are being used. Other than that little worry in the back of my mind, everyone who has driven the car has been overwhelmed with its performance and refinement. —JL

DODGE VIPER RT/10

going to be a V-8, how the first Viper test mule was fitted with a high-performance V-6, and how the Viper eventually ended up with a Lamborghini-revised all-aluminum version of an experimental Chrysler V-10 truck engine.

You have read all this because the public relations department, once it found something juicy to shake in front of the mad-dog press, shook that piece of snake meat for all it was worth. We have attended Viper planning meetings. We have been chauffeured in the car by Lutz. We have done hot laps at Indy with Shelby. And now the payoff. We get a spin behind the wheel.

(An aside: Now, I haven't minded attending all of these "off the record" Viper sessions for the past two years because they have been quite interesting, if somewhat time-consuming and unproductive from a reporter's standpoint. But I seriously mind the fact that *Road & Track* was not invited to drive the car as punishment for not playing along. Enough said.)

So much had been written about this blessed cartoon roadster before I actually warmed the Viper's fat little steering wheel in my own two hands that I'm not sure what else you need to know except, Is it any good? Good question.

24

A *big burble escaped when I goosed the throttle a bit, and the sound rumbled through my chest. Oooh, Lordy. I, of course, then stood on it.*

. . . .

Give me more.

As a beast, the Viper is a smashing success. "Bubba bubba," it said when I fired up the engine. A big burble escaped when I goosed the throttle a bit, and the sound rumbled through my chest. Oooh, Lordy. I, of course, then stood on it.

Torque is the Viper's calling card. Torque is the first and overriding sensation that you have when you nail the accelerator. It is there, all at once, nearly all 450 pounds-feet of it, from about 2000 rpm wiggling due east across the chart to almost 4800 rpm, and an overly heavy right foot will send up a cloud of smoky burnout.

What then? Well, I was barreling down the pavement in a rattletrap. Give me a more production-ready vehicle.

My first shot at a Viper, and I got the used Indy car with 2000 of the hardest miles a car could rack up. It rattled and the cowl shook and the hood shuddered as if it were fixing to rip from its moor-

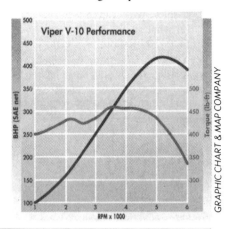

ROY SJOBERG

Executive Engineer, Viper Project

How did you land the plum job?
Bob Lutz called me into his office and said, "How would you like to head up Viper?" I'd had at least twenty-four hours to find out what a Viper was. I said, "I'd love it." He said, "You've got it." His only requirements were that it had to be ethical, and it had to be legal.

Was it your idea to pass around the list looking for car guys?
Yeah, that was my idea. Not loved by everyone. But car guys know each other. I never looked for an SCCA competition license, but I looked for enthusiasts. I looked for experienced people who could do things on their own, out of the corporate norm if needed. And I looked for people who had fire in their bellies.

What makes the Viper project special?
Viper, along with the LH platform, was our first platform team. Also, it was a chance to challenge Chrysler engineers to be system oriented, rather than component oriented. That has been a classic dilemma. Chrysler has had excellent components and mediocre automobiles. The focus of Lutz and [engineering vice-president] François Castaing is on producing excellent automobile engineers.

What about your specific goals?
The mission was to produce that automobile to the concept car's appearance, and to Cobra-like performance, in three years. That was it. We also wanted to develop training in vehicle and system engineering. We wanted a very small team. Life would have been easier with 200 people, but it would have been a lot harder to manage, so we started small.

Any special headaches?
I guess my number one headache has been cultural—the idea that hard work is enough. To Americans, effort is everything. To our international competition, results are everything. Every day, there is a supplier, an engineer, a guy in manufacturing, whatever, who is not delivering but who says, "Boy, I worked my ass off." When your competition relies on results, that's the only thing that will be good enough for you.

We are also in a high-volume mind-set. We are in a high-investment mind-set. We are in a high-resource mind-set. You have to break out of that and say, Wait a minute, this is different. Castaing's idea is to treat this like you've mortgaged your own home and this is *your* car company.

The third headache is that, every time we add someone new, every time we bring in new suppliers, we have to go through the whole mind-set thing again. It's not something you put to bed in the first month. You keep revisiting it and reinforcing it.

What are the advantages and disadvantages of the Viper's accelerated development pace?
You learn a lot fast. The disadvantages I hope I'll never know. We might find out in production. Have we covered everything our customers will do to the car? Probably not. Maybe they'll tow something. I wouldn't be a bit surprised to see a trailer or a motorhome behind a Viper.

There have been rumors that the car is a bear at the limit.
Yeah, there are rumors. On the positive side, it's great to have people talking about our car. On the negative side, we're absolutely baffled as to where all these experts are coming from. I've never seen so many people trying to help in a negative way. It's like having your neighbor say, before you even know, "I'm sorry your daughter's pregnant, and I'd like to help in any way I can." You don't need it. I knew this would happen with the Viper. It's a small group. Some people would like to be on it that didn't get on it. They will defecate on you. We are an irritant. It's the nature of the beast.

Did we like the handling of our first mule, the V-8? No. Did we like the handling of the first V-10 mule? You bet we liked it better. —JL

ings. I looked at the speedo and saw 65 mph. It felt like 100. At 100 mph, the engine roar sounded like I was sitting in the middle of a Chris-Craft; sand was blasting my cheeks; the wheel was tugging right and left in my hands; and the hood shake was scaring me.

But what an engine! I stepped on it, reading 120 mph on the speedo in fifth gear, seeing 3750 rpm on the tach, and wondering if the pressure and howl around my ears were going to explode my eardrums. I turned the wheel into a big, sweeping left-hander, and all the way through, the rear twitched and tugged like it wanted to step out.

And then they made me stop.

Give me more time at the wheel. Two lukewarm laps of *half* a patched and faded banked oval in each of two patched and faded prototypes only made me hot for more.

I thought I was really in the roses when I came back to a deserted proving ground a couple months later for a Sunday afternoon photo shoot. This time, the entire oval was open to me, but it was in such a state of disrepair that grass was growing up through the cracks in the cement. On the short and pitted straightaway, I actually braved the shuddering of the prototype all the way to 130 mph. But my blurred view of the rapidly approaching banking, with its tufts of quack grass poking through its split seams, had me pounding the brake pedal for a more circumspect entry onto its ragged, tilted surface. I racked up most of fifty miles on a slick skid-

DESIGN ANALYSIS

The toughest-looking car in production today.

If ever there was an object that looked the part it was intended to play, the brutal, inefficient, and tremendously exciting Dodge Viper is it. It was created purely as a show car—and then only because of a couple of minutes' conversation between Tom Gale and Bob Lutz during a chance meeting in a corridor in Highland Park in February 1988. When it appeared at the Detroit auto show in 1989, the Viper immediately attracted the kind of response every manufacturer dreams about: people waving checkbooks and demanding early delivery.

It's safe to say that the Viper's emergence as a 1992 production car is due, in large measure, to the tremendous enthusiasm of those who have lined up to buy the initial production run. Chrysler saw building it as a way to generate interest in the company during a dangerous time when it has no new products to offer, and when the old ones are desperately creaky. It's probably a good thing for the Viper that Chrysler is on the ropes, because in normal times it is extremely unlikely that any product so far removed from the mainstream would be built.

Chrysler design vice-president Tom Gale says that the Viper is basically the work of six or eight guys, although "a couple of dozen total put their hands on it." In Detroit-speak, that means this car is about as close to being the work of a single designer as ever happens in the Motor City. Gale won't single out the person who initially conceived the Viper, created in Neil Walling's Advanced Design department late in 1987, but he does credit Bob Hubbach with having done a lot of the final surface work and Ernie Barry and Ric Aneiros with having given it special attention borne of passion for the idea.

If those dates seem a little odd, it is because the designers wanted to do such a car *before* Bob Lutz uttered the fateful words, "We ought to do a Cobra car," in that hallway, and they'd already made a lot of sketches and full-size layouts. Gale had the first clay model made by an outside shop in Detroit, and then a refined fiberglass version was done at the Chrysler Pacifica facility in Carlsbad, California. That car was shorter, narrower, and had no roll bar, but it kept the initial character. If you study the published photos of various Viper prototypes, you'll see that the wheels have kept their three-cutter Cuisinart design but have lost a lot of the deep inset first shown because the engineers have stuffed in brake discs big enough for an eight-liter car.

A lot of refinement has taken place, but Gale is proud of the fact that the integrity of the initial concept has been retained. You can see that the grille tucks aft at the bottom now; the split between bumper and hood has been raised to run through the headlamp area; the driving lights are tunneled rather than covered; the mirrors are integrated into the windshield pillars; there is a metal rail on the top edge of the windshield; and so on. But none of the character has been dissipated.

I saw the Detroit show car as two separate designs brought together, the front and the back missing each other entirely, with a chrome exhaust system sitting in the misfitted gap between them holding the car together visually. That "gill" section no longer has the pipes, because there is too much risk for pedestrians and too much liability for Chrysler, but there is an honest air outlet in the space, the strong character line of the gill is preserved, and the exhaust system is evoked, if not exposed, along the sill.

There is an exiguous top but no roll-up windows, side curtains—as in the Cobra or the first Corvettes—being expected to do their usual inadequate job of keeping water out. More than anything else, more even than the giant engine, that one feature underlines the commitment to past ideas—and ideals—of what performance cars ought to be.

The Viper is not beautiful, not elegant, not particularly graceful or aerodynamic, but it is most certainly exactly what its creators and its clientele want. How often does anyone offer that virtue?

—Robert Cumberford

pad doing doughnuts for our lunatic photographer.

Give me more of a road to rip up. A real road. A real road trip. A real car. Ask me then how I feel about the Viper.

As I understand it, we will be driving production Vipers as you read this story. Until that time, I don't want to see another Viper. I don't want to see a *picture* of a Viper. I don't even want to hear the word "Viper." Get the job done, and we'll do the *real* drive stories when we have a real car to drive. 🛑

> **G**ive me more of a road to rip up. A real road. A real road trip. A real car. Ask me then how I feel about the Viper.
> ....

DODGE VIPER RT/10

GENERAL:
Front-engine, rear-wheel-drive roadster
2-passenger, 2-door composite body
Base price (estimated) $50,000 (+ luxury tax of 10% over $30,000 and estimated $4500 gas guzzler tax)

ENGINE:
OHV V-10, aluminum block and heads
Bore x stroke 4.00 x 3.88 in (101.6 x 98.5 mm)
Displacement 488 cu in (7997 cc)
Compression ratio 9.1:1
Fuel system sequential multipoint injection
Power SAE net 400 bhp @ 5200 rpm
Torque SAE net 450 lb-ft @ 3600 rpm
Redline 6000 rpm

DRIVETRAIN:
6-speed manual transmission
Gear ratios (I) 2.66 (II) 1.78 (III) 1.30 (IV) 1.00 (V) 0.74 (VI) 0.50
Final-drive ratio 3.07:1

MEASUREMENTS:
Wheelbase 96.2 in
Track front/rear 59.6/60.6 in
Length x width x height 175.1 x 75.7 x 44.0 in
Curb weight 3272 lb
Weight distribution front/rear 51/49%
Ground clearance 4.5 in
Coefficient of drag 0.50
Fuel capacity 22.0 gal

SUSPENSION:
Independent front, with double A-arms, adjustable dampers, anti-roll bar
Independent rear, with double A-arms, adjustable dampers, anti-roll bar

STEERING:
Rack-and-pinion
Turns lock to lock 2.4
Turning circle 40.7 ft

BRAKES:
Vented discs front and rear

WHEELS AND TIRES:
17 x 10.0-in front, 17 x 13.0-in rear cast aluminum wheels
275/40ZR-17 front, 335/35ZR-17 rear Michelin XGT2 tires

PERFORMANCE (manufacturer's data):
0–60 mph in 4.0 sec
0–100 mph in 14.0 sec
Top speed 165 mph
Pounds per bhp 8.2
City driving (estimated) 15 mpg

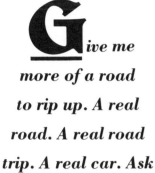

DRIVING THE NEW CARS

DODGE VIPER

Standing one metre away, you feel the heavy metal breathing of its 300 kW, eight-litre V10. Jukka Sihvonen was one of the first journalists to get his hands on the car Bob Lutz described as 'an exciting, gut-wrenching, out-and-out sports car with no frills'...

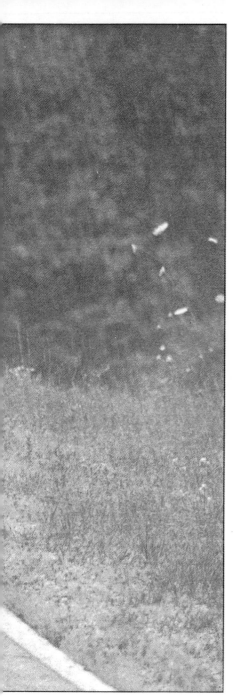

Touted by its Chrysler creators as the 'nineties successor to the Cobra, the Viper exudes power rather than elegance: a 44 magnum styling statement that makes no apologies to Pininfarina.

STANDING one metre from the Dodge Viper, one can feel the heavy-metal breathing of its 300 kilowatt, eight-litre V10. The driver nudges the throttle and the exhaust rushing from the huge sidepipes whumps you, just about crotch level.

That is wonderfully appropriate. After all, that is precisely where Dodge has aimed the Viper. This is not a cerebral, high-tech engineering exercise. The Viper is old-time religion — a visceral experience at modern-day prices.

The original Viper made its debut (as a concept vehicle) at the North American Automobile Show in 1989. Since then, the Viper Gang of Three — Chrysler poohbah Bob Lutz, Chrysler engineering director Francois Castaing and Chrysler chief stylist Tom Gale — have been Viper-active, enthusiastically touting the two-seater as the 'nineties successor to the Cobra.

"Sports cars have gotten way too East Coast, effete... effeminate, with lots of whizzy little parts in there and way too much electronics and too much sophistication," declared Lutz in 1989. The Viper he envisioned would be a "true sports car... an exciting, gut-wrenching, basic automobile with no frills... a connection of man and machine with a minimum of complication."

Using an 85-strong team including engineers, designers, manufacturing, finance and purchasing agents and employing simultaneous engineering, the Viper is being brought to market in what is for Chrysler record time — just under 36 months. The development costs are estimated at 20 million US dollars, with another 50 million set aside for tooling and manufacturing costs.

Some Chrysler executives, including Lutz, believe that the fact that more than a year was cut off Chrysler's normal development time may be the most significant thing about the Viper. The car is now scheduled to go on sale in the United States in early 1992 with about 200 cars built the first year.

After that, volume may increase to as much as 3 000 a year and there are plans to sell cars in Europe early in 1993. "What we want is to go and challenge the Germans on their home ground," says Jean Mallebay Vacquer, Chrysler's general manager of special projects' engineering.

A pair of prototypes

On a fine, warm day at Chrysler's proving grounds in Michigan, after two years of public relations foreplay, it is finally time for the first non-Chrysler employees to drive a pair of Viper prototypes. One had been driven by ex-racer and Viper enthusiast Carroll Shelby as the pace car at the 1991 Indianapolis 500. The other is a slightly ragged development car. They are worth about 300 000 dollars each. There is still some fine-tuning to be done, but Chrysler officials insist the pair are very close to what production models will be like.

The Viper's appearance has changed little from the 1989 concept car. It is still attention getting, purposeful and anything but delicate or understated.

This is no quietly elegant Pininfarina design. This is a 44 magnum styling statement that passes "strong" and moves into "blatant", further accentuated by a somewhat silly decal of a snake on the bonnet. One could drive forever in a ZR1 Corvette and only the cognoscenti would notice. But even Stevie Wonder would never miss a Viper.

The overall length is 4 369 mm, arranged over a 2 438 mm wheelbase. The Viper, which will be built in Detroit, has a rectangular tube frame with plastic composite body panels formed with low-pressure moulding and affixed with mechanical fasteners.

The interior is as basic as the concept. Air-conditioning won't even be available, despite a price described by straight-faced Chrysler spokesmen as "hopefully under 50 000 dollars." The unspoken attitude suggests that the Viper is a driver's car and creature-comfort seeking sissies should spend their disposable income elsewhere.

The tachometer and speedometer are large. Black on white. Simple, with the speedometer reading 180 mph. Glance to the right a bit and there's information on coolant temperature, oil pressure, fuel level and volts.

There is an AM/FM radio/cassette, with the speakers located between the seats, facing forward. Tweeters are located in the doors. There is a snap-in soft top that can be stored in the smallish boot, but as of now it had yet to be tested for high-speed "viability".

There is no airbag. Instead, Chrysler will require Viper-isti to clamber beneath a door-mounted "passive" system required to meet federal safety regulations. However, it plans to provide mounting hardware for those who would like five-point racing harnesses.

The seats are comfortable, but adjustments are limited to fore-and-aft and seatback rake.

The foot room is also tight, with nearness of the wheel meaning there is no dead pedal. That leaves tall drivers wondering where to store the left foot when it is not pushing up and down, driving what Chrysler hopes will be the Lord of the Flyers. The good news is that the pedals are nicely aligned, for those of the heel-and-toe persuasion.

V10 'wants out'...

Even at idle, the V10 shakes the Viper. Lots. It is as if something really big and not particularly refined is trapped under the hood and is moderately serious about wanting out. This engine, after all, is based on a V10 truck engine Chrysler plans to introduce on a new pick-up. But instead of being annoying, the vibro-massage seems somehow in keeping with the Viper's persona.

The clutch take-up is sharp, the pressure moderately heavy but not so severe that it will substitute for Nautilus. Not surprisingly, the Viper's acceleration is immensely adequate and equally immediate.

Chrysler claims the V10, with its

9,5:1 compression and multi-point fuel injection, produces 300 kW at 4 600 r/min and 610 N.m of torque at 3 200 r/min. It uses a 3,07:1 Dana final drive. The current kerb weight is about 1 454 kg. That is 91 kg over the target weight and Dodge plans to introduce the Viper at this figure and trim some mass off later.

Chrysler was not allowing our small group any "instrumented testing". But they claim that even at its overly chubby weight, the Viper meets its goals.

They are: zero-to-60 mph (96,6 km/h) in four seconds, zero-to-100 mph (161 km/h) and back to zero in 14,5 seconds, top speed of 257 km/h, a quarter mile at 12,7 seconds and pulling 1,0 Gs on a 91,4 m skid pad.

The six-speed gearbox is a Borg-Warner design, chosen after a Getrag unit was dumped over what Chrysler said were "economic issues". The pattern is identical to a conventional five-speed, with sixth straight down and reverse available up and to the right of fifth.

The shift lever is light and a little notchy, but quite acceptable. But with so much torque, those who shun manual labour can almost use the six-speed as an automatic.

After all, Chrysler claims the all-aluminium, 20-valve V10 is already producing 542 N.m of torque at 1 600 r/min and my driving impressions make that assessment seem quite reasonable.

Get hard on the throttle, which is how the designers intend the Viper to be driven, and any opportunity for conversation ends, eliminated by an engine/exhaust duet. It is a deep noise, distinctive but not sounding as raucously sophisticated as a Porsche 911.

Under full throttle acceleration, Viper Sound can easily be heard 400 metres away. That is one of the problems that worries Viper engineers, when they prepare to market the car in Europe. The acceptable limits are low.

"Switzerland is our worst, 75 decibels," says one Viper engineer during a staff meeting later that day. "75 decibels? Can we shut the engine off and coast through (the test)?" responds Chrysler powertrain expert Chris Theodore.

Another major change for Euro-bound Vipers involves the side exhaust pipes. The American version used pressure-formed Nomex with stainless steel cladding to reduce the chances of the unwary being burned. Chrysler believes such sidepipes would be illegal in Europe, so the exhaust will be routed traditionally.

With a V10 hunkered down up front, one expects the Viper to be nose-heavy. Wrong. Chrysler has adopted a front mid-ship design that pushes the V10 165 mm behind the axle.

That requires the pedals to be skewed slightly to the left, but the design provides a 50/50 weight distribution. Particularly for its size, the Viper is remarkably eager to change directions, offering a surprisingly sharp turn-in. The steering is tight, if slightly uncommunicative. It is willing to obey, but not

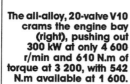

The all-alloy, 20-valve V10 crams the engine bay (right), pushing out 300 kW at only 4 600 r/min and 610 N.m of torque at 3 200, with 542 N.m available at 1 600.

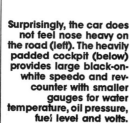

Surprisingly, the car does not feel nose heavy on the road (left). The heavily padded cockpit (below) provides large black-on-white speedo and rev-counter with smaller gauges for water temperature, oil pressure, fuel level and volts.

chatty.

There was a slight but noticeable difference in steering feel between the two vehicles, the result of on-going development work. Some drivers felt one was slightly loose. The vehicle I drove, however, was fine.

The suspension is fully independent, using short-long arms, coil springs over Koni shocks and front and rear stabiliser bars. Through a cone-marked road course, the Viper's body motions were tightly controlled with minimal body lean and the structural rigidity felt good. On the smooth surfaces Chrysler chose for our drive however, both ride quality and scuttle shake remained question marks.

Although one hesitates to flail about excessively in one of two such expensive prototypes, the grip seemed impressive and the Viper is likely to be yet another sports car whose capabilities wildly exceed those of most of its drivers. Part of that adhesion is thanks to God's little acre of rubber underneath. The Viper uses Michelin's XGT-Zs with 275/40/17s up front and 335/35/17s in the rear.

Move into a left-hand sweeper at about 130 km/h and back off the throttle. The tail moves slightly wide but the movement is quite benign. Helpful, not threatening. The nose edges a little deeper into the turn but understeer still dominates. "Because we can't control who is going to buy it, we are trying to develop a vehicle that is not going to get the driver in trouble," explains Viper engineer Herb Helbig.

One driver complains that the other prototype, the one he drives, is light and twitchy at the tail. But that is not the case with ours.

A tight, decreasing radius comes up. The Viper's brakes are 330 mm ventilated discs, front and rear, with the fronts using a four-piston caliper. The pedal brake has a take-no-prisoners firmness.

It feels like serious stopping power, but none of that new fangled stuff from Teves or Bosch. "We have no anti-lock, just big brakes," says one Viper engineer.

At the engineering meeting later, Chrysler engineers will discuss the hard pads and the probability that at some time, the Viper's brakes will simply and rudely squeal. Rather than change the brakes, they are seriously considering putting a notice in the owner's manual that the Viper is a performance car and the noise is normal. Take two aspirins and don't call your dealer in the morning...

A few more laps and it is time to get out of the Viper. Is America's next sports car going to match up to the Viper-hype? Can one justify a 50 000 dollar tag for a sports car without increasingly common technology such as all-wheel drive, rear-wheel steer, traction control, an adaptive suspension or even anti-lock brakes?

The answer will take more quality time behind the wheel and with finished vehicles, not prototypes. But finding out is going to be fun. ●

DODGE
VIPER RT/10

Dodge builds a Cobra for the Nineties

PHOTOS BY BRIAN BLADES

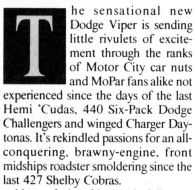

The sensational new Dodge Viper is sending little rivulets of excitement through the ranks of Motor City car nuts and MoPar fans alike not experienced since the days of the last Hemi 'Cudas, 440 Six-Pack Dodge Challengers and winged Charger Daytonas. It's rekindled passions for an all-conquering, brawny-engine, front midships roadster smoldering since the last 427 Shelby Cobras.

No confusing this wonderfully outrageous red 2-seater with some VW-powered kit car or Japanese techno-marvel. When is the last time an American car, let alone one from Chrysler, has caused such a stir?

Why? For starters, the Viper's visage is imposing. A menacing wide-mouth grille and animalistic polyellipsoid headlamps look as though they just made a long journey up the River Styx. Here and there, hints of the Viper's inspirational forebear, the Shelby Cobra 427, are recognizable: in the curved haunches of the rear fenders, in the basic honesty of the instrument panel, in the muscular bulges of the hood and front fenders.

The Viper sits low and wide, as if ready to uncoil with explosive force at a moment's notice. At 75.7 in., it's wider than a Corvette ZR-1 or Ferrari 348. Standing just 44.0 in. high, the Viper's squatter than a Ferrari F40 or Testarossa, and more than 2-1/2 in. lower than the Acura NSX.

Reptilian gill-like vents at the rear edge of the front fenders give a hint of the massive V-10 engine that lies under the Viper's hood and are functional heat-exchangers, too. The crowning bad-to-the-bone touch is the side-mounted exhaust pipes, (Vipers sold in the state of Connecticut and 1993 models exported to Europe will have a rear-exit exhaust).

A targa-like structural bar hints of the roadster version of the Ford GT40. Flying in the face of more sophisticated exotics with their climate-controlled cockpits, the open-air nature of the Viper validates the notion that the pleasures of driving it are of this Earth.

Light on the acouterments, heavy

on the performance hardware, the Viper is about as different from traditional Chrysler fare (K-Cars, minivans, vinyl-roof New Yorkers and Jeeps) as possible. A scant 200 cars will be produced in model year 1992. By 1993, planned production rises to 2000 cars, sales to Europe beginning as well. Ultimately, Chrysler says it can build 3000-5000 Vipers per year, but that may be pegging the size of the open, 2-seat near-exotic niche optimistically. Initially, anyway, a 2-year Viper waiting list and stiff dealer premiums are a near certainty.

As with the Cobra and numerous classic British roadsters, there are no outside door handles; you reach inside and with a backhanded flip, pull open the inside door release handle. That long black object your pant leg is making contact with is the engine exhaust sidepipe, and just upstream of it is one of the car's two catalytic converters. If the car's been running recently, it's best to stay clear.

A short, easy hike over the sill and sidepipes and you alight in a supportive, no-nonsense bucket seat that seems to fit drivers short or tall, large or small. Aside from the pipes, ingress and egress is much easier than in, say, a Corvette or any number of high-dollar exotics. There are but two adjustments, seatback rake and fore/aft. The federally mandated passive restraints are door-mounted belts with well-located outboard anchor points. The footwell is not cramped, but because the pedals are shifted to the left to clear the front midships engine configuration, there's no room left for a clutch dead pedal.

Seated at the controls, a leather-wrapped, 3-spoke steering wheel of robust construction beckons you to the open road. There's a wonderfully simple yet attractive instrument layout with 7000-rpm tachometer, 180-mph speedometer and warning-lamp binnacles centered in front of the driver. The one obvious concession to Sybaritic conduct, a 6-speaker AM/FM stereo cassette, which Chrysler wags insist is enjoyable to listen to up to 100 mph.

The Viper has a high driveline tunnel, which also houses structural members that help account for its outstanding 5000 lb-ft per degree torsional stiffness. Sprouting somewhat awkwardly out of the tunnel is the handbrake, and the 6-speed shifter. The Viper's shifter has relatively long throws, but easy-to-find, precise gates.

The Viper shuns outside door handles, roll-up side windows and factory-installed air conditioning, but a portable canvas convertible top and side curtains are standard equipment. Stowed in the trunk, the top is supported by 5 steel bows running laterally and the entire mechanism expands accordian-like to stretch and latch in place between the windshield header and roof structural bar. The "window" part of the side curtains is see-through, flexible vinyl, like that used for the rear window on many convertible tops. At the leading edge of each curtain is a flap that can be pushed open to gain access to the door release handle inside the cockpit.

A first on a modern production car is Viper's all-aluminum V-10 engine. This 400-bhp, 8.0-liter (488 cu-in.) powerplant is the Viper's heart and soul. Derived from a similar V-10 of the same displacement with cast-iron heads and block that will debut in Dodge trucks in 1993, the Viper V-10's architecture is essentially that of Chrysler's small-block 5.9-liter (360 cu-in.) V-8 with two cylinders added.

As with the 427 Cobra, the Viper V-10's long suit is prodigious torque—something large-displacement, pushrod-actuated, 2-valve-per-cylinder engines are very effective at generating. Though it peaks with 450 lb-ft at 3600 rpm, the V-10's torque curve is a broad plateau extending from 1500 to 5500 rpm. A sequential multi-point fuel injection system with bottom-fed injectors, dual throttle bodies and dual plenums provides excellent driveability and tuned intake runners give a ram-tuning effect between 2000 and 4000 rpm.

Fire up the engine, and the cerebral bench racing fades in favor of gutsy excitement. Because of the uneven firing pulses (occuring at 90 and 54 degrees of crankshaft rotation), the exhaust note is sort of a macho staccato chugga-chugga with

a slight wheeze. The Viper's phonics won't remind you of Sebring, 1966, or the NHRA Winternationals, or Talladega or even today's Bob's Big Boy on a Saturday night.

An all-new Borg-Warner T56 6-speed transmission and hydraulically actuated 12-in. clutch gets this Monster of the MoPar Midway in gear and down the road in a hurry. The Borg-Warner engineers claim to have paid special attention to gear-tooth microfinish and gear spacing. The result is a truly modern, quiet, easy-shifting close-ratio transmission with two overdrive gears, not at all like the cement-mixer sound Corvette's ZF 6-speed is sometimes likened to. And the Viper's box has a computer-aided 1-to-4 shift to help with the EPA city cycle fuel mileage rating (thereby minimizing the gas-guzzler tax). No automatic transmission is offered or somehow appropriate in the Viper. Aft of the gearbox, a short aluminum driveshaft goes to a limited-slip 3.07:1 Dana 44 differential.

The Viper slithers forth wearing a composite skin formed largely by the resin transfer molding (RTM) process. Underneath the Viper's sinewy skin is a surprisingly rigid tubular steel backbone frame. The Viper's stout skeleton provides a solid platform for the chassis components to do their fancy footwork. During 2 days and over 300 miles of aggressive driving over a variety of road surfaces, I could not detect any cowl shake or steering column shake and only a minimum amount of movement of the doors in their frames.

As befits a classic sports car, the Viper sports fully independent suspension, with unequal-length upper and lower control arms at each corner. A pair of stabilizing toe links are used with the rear lower control arms. Low-pressure gas-charged Koni coil-over damper/spring assemblies and front and rear anti-roll bars round out the underpinnings. Steering is power-assisted rack and pinion and it offers good on-center feel. Response is immediate.

Part and parcel of the Viper's animalistic aura is a huge 17-in. tire and aluminum wheel package. The rear skins, Michelin XGT P335/35ZR-17s, are more than a foot wide, larger than the Corvette ZR-1s and the same size as the Diablos.

Inboard lie monster brakes, 13-in. vented discs with Brembo calipers. No ABS is available. Chrysler worked very hard to build a hands-on machine that matches or betters the performance of the mythological 427 Cobra. One of the bogies foremost in the minds of the Chrysler engineers was the Cobra's vaunted 0-100-0-mph time of 15.0 sec. The Viper guys claim their snake can do it in 14.5 seconds.

But let's not kid ourselves. The Viper isn't about numbers. It's unbridled emotion on wheels. It's about explosive locomotion and the power to blast to 100 or 150 mph at will without working up a sweat. It's about balance and a 50/50 weight distribution that lets a skilled driver arm wrestle difficult corners, approach and dance on the edge of the laws of physics without computer intervention. With a deep and abiding well of torque, you can accelerate out of corners faster and with the massive binders, it's possible to brake later.

Strapped into the Viper's passenger seat alongside Cobra sire, Carroll Shelby, at Willow Springs Raceway, I just had to ask him if he ever dreamed a car as exciting as his 427 Cobra would be built again. He just half-turned, smiled broadly and shook his head no as we entered a series of delicious sweepers. Sometimes when you're driving the Dodge Viper RT/10, non-verbal forms of communication are all that's necessary.

—*Ron Sessions*

DODGE VIPER RT/10

PRICE
List price, all POE . . . . est $50,000   Price as tested . . . . .est $52,600
Price as tested includes std equip. (Chrysler/Alpine AM/FM stereo/cassette, tilt steering column, tonneau cover, security alarm system, leather seat trim, removable fabric top, side curtains & rear window), gas guzzler tax (est. $2600)

ENGINE
Type	ohv 2-valve V-10
Displacement	7990 cc
Bore x stroke	101.6 mm x 98.6 mm
Compression ratio	9.1:1
Horsepower, (SAE)	400 bhp @ 4600 rpm
Torque	450 lb-ft @ 3600 rpm
Maximum engine speed	6000 rpm
Fuel injection	electronic sequential multi-port
Fuel requirement	unleaded, 92 pump oct

GENERAL
Curb weight	est 3300 lb
Test weight	na
Weight dist, f/r, %	50/50
Wheelbase	96.2 in.
Track, f/r	59.6 in./60.6 in.
Length	175.1 in.
Width	75.7 in.
Height	44.0 in.
Trunk space	est 9.0 cu ft

DRIVETRAIN
Transmission . . . . 6-sp manual

Gear	Ratio	Overall ratio	(Rpm) Mph
1st	2.66:1	8.17:1	(6000) 56
2nd	1.78:1	5.46:1	(6000) 83
3rd	1.30:1	3.99:1	(6000) 114
4th	1.00:1	3.07:1	(6000) 148
5th	0.74:1	2.27:1	est (4950) 165
6th	0.50:1	1.54:1	est (3360) 165

Final drive ratio 3.07:1
Engine rpm @ 60 mph in 6th . . . . 1220 rpm

CHASSIS & BODY
Layout	front engine/rear drive
Body/frame	RTM fiberglass/tubular steel
Brakes	13.0-in. vented discs, vacuum assist
Wheels	alloy, 17 x 10-in f/17 x 13-in r
Tires	P275/40ZR-17 f/ P335/35ZR-17 r
Steering	rack & pinion, power assist
Turns, lock to lock	2.4
Suspension, f/r	upper & lower A-arms, coil-over shocks, anti-roll bar/upper & lower A-arms, toe links, coil-over shocks, anti-roll bar

HANDLING
Lateral accel (200-ft skidpad) . . . . . . est 0.95g

ACCELERATION
Time to speed	Seconds
0–60 mph	est 4.5
Time to distance	
0–1320 ft (¼ mi)	est 12.9 sec @ 113 mph

FUEL ECONOMY
EPA combined	est 16 mpg
Fuel capacity	22.0 gal.

BRAKING
From 60 mph	est 119 ft
From 80 mph	est 211 ft

ROAD TEST DODGE VIPER RT/10

FINALLY, THE LAST VIPER STORY YOU'LL HAVE TO READ (FOR A WHILE)

by Jeff Karr

PHOTOGRAPHY BY RICK GRAVES

By now, you're probably sick of the Dodge Viper RT/10. Never in modern times has a single vehicle received so much advance attention from the media. Dodge's redraft of the classic '60s muscle-car has been in the spotlight every inch of the way on the trip from showcar to showroom. There's likely not a single element of its creation that hasn't been dealt with in full detail. About a hundred times.

At *Motor Trend*, we've done at least our share of Viper-related coverage, and with good reason. For what it represents to the enthusiast driver and the future of the domestic auto industry, the Viper is news. Not because it points in a new or meaningful technical direction: It's underlying concept is and always has been an engineering

dead-end. No, the meaning behind the Viper lies in the spirit behind the car and in the method and swiftness with which it progressed from a wildly whimsical show car into an almost equally wild production car.

In a world where, as a rule, beautiful show cars mutate into bland parodies of themselves by the time they reach production, the Viper has made it to showrooms with nearly all its original venom intact. The result is a car that can upstage anything on wheels, wherever it goes. In the mold of the original Shelby Cobra, the Viper was to be a simple two-seater with a ton of power and only the most rudimentary creature comforts. The Viper makes the weather-tight Ferrari F-40 and Lamborghini Diablo seem positively sensible by comparison.

The hood is a challenge to open, but well worth the effort. The V-10 isn't really sophisticated in its technology, but it most certainly *is* in its power delivery. No excuses, no waiting; it's like having your right foot wired directly up to God's own adrenaline pump. While you're at it, you might want to ask His help in getting the hood shut again. You'll need it.

You'll want to replace the silly, door-mounted three-point belts with the dealer-option five-point harnesses before you even take delivery. First stop on the way home should be the nearest Thrifty Drug Store, where you'll need sunscreen (for obvious reasons), earplugs (buffeting in the cabin is substantial at speed), and a few cheap baseball caps (they blow off every time you hit redline in third).

The list of comfort and convenience features not found on the Viper is a long and complete one. Highlights of the not present and definitely unaccounted for include outside door latches, side glass, power mirrors, and air conditioning. There are also key technical features you can forget about, too, like multiple camshafts and four-valve heads, turbochargers, traction-control, anti-lock brakes, and an airbag.

Due, at least in part, to these notable omissions, the driving experience is unique among modern automobiles. The Viper's doors are opened by reaching inside the car and pulling the release handle. Locks are provided, but they're meant to satisfy some obscure DOT regulation and aren't expected to foil any save the dimmest of thieves. A key-chain-controlled alarm system provides a small measure of security and should give Viper owners the courage to leave sight of their car for short periods of time. In good neighborhoods. In daylight.

Once settled into the driver's seat, you'll find a comfortable but distinctly odd driving environment. The pedals are grouped far to the left to provide room for the engine. The effort levels of the brake and clutch pedals are firm, but not unpleasantly so. Nicely supportive leather-faced seats have a manual seatback angle adjuster and a squeeze-bulb type lumbar support adjuster. You also can set the steering wheel angle to suit your whims, so it's not too hard to come to terms with the car. Plainly visible, white-faced instruments tell you everything worth knowing in a classic, simple format.

The only remotely superfluous item in the interior is the six-speaker stereo system. It's reasonably good when the car is at rest, but wind turbulence and the exhaust drone nearly drown it out at high speeds. In terms of style points, the businesslike matte-finish dashboard comes across as clean and aggressive to some drivers, and simply cheap to others. The flimsy feel of the glovebox door met with disfavor, as did the fit of the door panels. The various interior bits are undergoing continuous refinement on the assembly line, according to Dodge; our test car was serial number 11, and there's still room for improvement.

Once underway, you'll notice plenty of heat in the footwells, on the coolant temperature gauge, and through the interior air vents. Don't worry about the engine; an auxiliary fan kicks in to keep things from boiling over. Do worry about your own composure, though. Heat is everywhere in the Viper. Watch the sidepipes and the smoking-hot (literally) doorsills when getting in or out. Learn to live with the 10 to 15 degrees of unwanted heat put into the vent system, or pay your dealer to install the optional air conditioner. Until you do, pray you never get caught in a summer thunderstorm. If you put on the cumbersome and leaky vinyl top and side curtains (which completely fill the trunk when stowed, by the way), you'll be trapped in a claustrophobic steam chamber that'll have you desperately scooping handfuls of cool air through the narrow zippered slits in the side curtains.

You wouldn't expect a roofless car to be any trouble to see out from, but the Team Viper people have defied physics this time out. The narrow-angle sideview mirrors are your best bet, but they have to be adjusted by hand—a task just as tedious today as it was back in the '60s with the original Cobra. The center mirror mostly shows you the B-pillar support bar behind the seats: Patrolmen will soon learn that a Viper is best approached from directly behind.

Particularly in freeway traffic, the Dodge is perennially at the center of a small traffic jam of onlookers, clotting main travel arteries like some sort of high-test coagulant. Busting loose of gangs of waving rubberneckers is no problem, however, given the V-10's daunting torque reserves.

Even at a mere 1200 rpm in sixth gear (about 60 mph), the Viper responds smartly to any application of throttle. That top cog only exists to squeeze a reasonable 22 highway mpg out of the car to please the feds; it's a safe bet people who've just dropped over 50 grand to buy The Most Useless Car In America aren't really concerned with fuel mileage. Better to keep the Dodge percolating along at about 2000 rpm or more, where the gratifying mount of thrust available is clearly worth the price of admission. Find a nice piece of snaking road, and you can just leave it in third for a whole tankful of gas. The Viper jumps off corners like nothing else; peaky, finicky turbos and little four-valve motors just can't equal the instantaneous and downright wonderful surge the Viper delivers.

And though the V-10 finds its roots in a future Chrysler truck engine, the help Lamborghini provided in its adaptation here makes it anything but a slow-witted foot soldier. The V-10 revs out to its 6000-rpm redline without running short of motivation. Ultimately, though, it's the Viper's overall flexibility that makes it thoroughly unique. There's power everywhere; you don't have to go looking for it, because it'll come looking for you.

The Viper's hard performance is always a crowd pleaser, but the audio/visceral presentation doesn't always play to rave reviews. The exhaust note at the impossibly low 400-rpm idle has the muffled, burbling cadence of a well-worn motorboat. At mid revs, there's a sonorous resonance between the two side pipes (each handling five cylinders) that has an aggressive edge, yet an "edited for airline use" sterility takes some of the sting out.

But at high engine speed, there's no debate, the Viper makes its best sounds. It's sort of an urgent, breathy hiss—the sound of a great volume of spent gasses spraying overboard at what sounds like incredible pressure. It's nothing like the uncorked bellow of a classic big-block Cobra, but in its way, the Viper's throaty hiss has a scary character all its own. It sounds like nothing you've ever heard, but some-

thing in your genetic makeup tells you its a dangerous sound. Be afraid.

Not many cars will outstrike the Viper. In our Feb. '92 issue, we recorded a ZR-1 Vette-beating 4.8-second trip from 0-60 in the Viper; that was in a prototype car at a place other than our normal test venue. For this article, at our normal track, the Viper used just 4.7 seconds to make the same trip; that's a tenth quicker than the number generated in a Callaway Twin Turbo for the August '91 issue, but not as quick as the best-ever ZR-1 time (4.3 seconds) we recorded a couple years ago. It stacks up well against the "brand-new" Shelby 427 S/C Cobra also tested in this issue, virtually mirroring its performance. Not bad for breathing through converters and real mufflers. The Viper could be quicker with more off-the line grip and quicker shift action from the otherwise agreeable Borg-Warner six-speed.

In a full quarter-mile run, the Viper stacks up about the same. It betters the ZR-1 by a small margin, but barely trails the Callaway: 13.0 seconds/112.7 mph versus 13.1/108.8 for the Viper. The Viper isn't the absolute quickest thing you can buy, but it certainly runs with a fast crowd.

As impressive as the Viper's performance under acceleration is, the chassis' handling numbers must be considered no less stirring. Our car made 0.97 g of lateral acceleration on the skidpad without great drama and hardly a scrap of body roll. The 50/50 weight distribution serves the Viper well, and the car is nearly neutral as it reaches the limits of its considerable grip. The cornering attitude is completely up to the driver, however. Get up to the limit, then lift off or step down sharply with your right foot, and the rear end will swing out into a glorious slide. Watch your steering closely though; the Viper lacks the catchable feel of a Vette or Nissan 300ZX when in heavy opposite-lock situations. The Viper's absolutely linear engine response will help a talented driver overcome the car's remote steering feel when playing on the skidpad, but not without some practice.

The same can be said of the Dodge's manners in the slalom. While the car's 68.4-mph average speed through the 600-foot course is good, the Viper isn't a car quickly mastered. You can bust loose its giant 335/35ZR17 rear Michelin XGT Zs at any point on the course. To drive the car well, new shadings of throttle control must be mastered; a ZR-1 is simple to drive in comparison.

The darker side of the Viper's nature is only truly apparent on the test track where you can explore big slip angles and arm-flailing oversteer. The car has an excellent chassis, extremely rigid and well suspended. But it's a classic Cobra-class muscle-car, and as such, requires high levels of driver skill and prescience if you wish to successfully venture over the limit. The Viper has no handy "eject" handle, no stabilizing ABS like most modern sports cars; misdirect the Viper's 400 horsepower or 3280 pounds at a bad moment, and you will be bitten. No car is foolproof, least of all the Viper.

On regular roads where smoother, saner tactics are the order, the Viper is a great treat to drive. The grip is positively tremendous, and, for the most part, shifting can be ignored. The steering, though hardly rich with information, at least has a solid, progressive feel, and the Viper turns in sharply and with hardly a hint of body roll. The wide, progressive Michelins are kept planted by the Viper's double wishbone suspension in most situations. Like other big-tired, firmly sprung cars, though, the Viper's composure is disrupted by genuinely rough or uneven pavement. The basic structure seems stout, much more so than most open cars, but when you really bound over bumpy surfaces, there are some secondary wiggles and squeaks in the bodywork, but no signs of protest from the tubular steel frame. The brakes are strong and fade resistant, but can be a little tough to modulate well at the point of lockup. Our best stop of 145 feet from 60 mph suggests the bias could still use a bit more tuning, or that ABS can't arrive too soon for future Vipers. There are many aspects of Cobra-class cars that are well worth reliving, but non-anti-lock brakes aren't among them.

The Viper is truth in advertising incarnate. Just as originally promised, the car's appeal is strictly visceral and emo-

With immense 17-inch Michelin XGT Zs front and rear, pizza-pan-size 13-inch vented disc brakes, and bulging fenders, the powerful Viper makes no secret of its intentions. In person, it's downright scary-looking.

tional. What the Viper offers is an 8-liter V-10 engine and just enough structure to lash one happy passenger on either side of its whirling driveshaft. To the people responsible for the Viper, nothing else really seemed necessary.

And it won't to the approximately 200 first-year Viper owners, either. All the stuff they're looking for is here, and not a bit more. The car's Spartan nature is at the heart of its appeal; some people will lapse into a happy adrenal spasm when they slide behind the Viper's wheel; others will wonder when they can park this breezy carnival ride and get into a real car.

Those complainers are the people who simply don't get it. Why you'd spend so much money to suffer such discomfort and inconvenience escapes them. If you've read this far, you probably know exactly why. Nothing you can drive packs the personality, makes the statement, or snaps your neck like the Dodge Viper RT/10. Nothing at all. **MT**

SECOND OPINION

Though more an entertainment device for affluent semi-adults than a car, the Viper is the most significant American automobile in decades. Yet its importance has nothing to do with its blazing acceleration, race-car handling, or styling that draws attention like Harrison Ford in the express line at Safeway. Instead, the Viper's distinction lies in how it was conceived, designed, and produced.

With the Viper, Chrysler tossed out Detroit's previous ponderous system, a practice that had (and has) as little hope of catching the Japanese as does a LeBaron of running down a Viper. With the Viper, Chrysler's top brass assembled its best and brightest, gave them an appropriate budget, and turned them loose.

The fruit of Team Viper beats a Ferrari 512TR in most performance parameters, is more fun to drive, *and* will attract more envious glances—at less than a third the cost. —*Mac DeMere*

TECH DATA
Dodge Viper RT/10

GENERAL
Make and model ....Dodge Viper RT/10
Manufacturer..Chrysler Corp., Detroit, Mich.
Location of final assembly plant....................Detroit, Mich.
Body style 2-door, 2-passenger
Drivetrain layout ....Front engine, rear drive
Base price..$50,000
Price as tested..$53,300
Options included..None
Ancillary charges ....Gas-guzzler tax, $2600; destination, $700
Typical market competition........Chevrolet Corvette ZR-1, Acura NSX, Porsche 968

DIMENSIONS
Wheelbase, in./mm 96.2/2444
Track, f/r, in./mm 59.6/60.6/1514/1539
Length, in./mm 175.1/4448
Width, in./mm..75.7/1923
Height, in./mm..43.9/1115
Ground clearance, in./mm 5.1/130
Manufacturer's curb weight, lb 3280
Weight distribution, f/r, % 50/50
Cargo capacity, cu ft 11.8
Fuel capacity, gal 22.0
Weight/power ratio, lb/hp..8.2

ENGINE
Type ....V-10, liquid cooled, cast aluminum block and heads
Bore x stroke, in./mm..4.00 x 3.88/ 101.6 x 98.6
Displacement, ci/cc 488/7990
Compression ratio 9.1:1
Valve gear ....OHV, 2 valves/cylinder
Fuel/induction system..................................Multipoint EFI
Horsepower
  hp @ rpm, SAE net ....400 @ 4600
Torque
  lb-ft @ rpm, SAE net ....450 @ 3600
Horsepower/liter 50.1
Redline, rpm 6000
Recommended fuel ....Unleaded premium

DRIVELINE
Transmission type..6-speed man.
Gear ratios
  (1st) 2.66:1
  (2nd) 1.78:1
  (3rd) 1.30:1
  (4th) 1.00:1
  (5th) 0.74:1
  (6th) 0.50:1
Axle ratio 3.07:1
Final-drive ratio..1.54:1
Engine rpm,
  60 mph in top gear 1200

CHASSIS
Suspension
Front......................Upper and lower control arms, coil springs, anti-roll bar
Rear.......................Upper and lower control arms, coil springs, anti-roll bar
Steering
Type................................Rack and pinion, power assist
Ratio 16.7:1
Turns, lock to lock 2.4
Turning circle 40.7
Brakes
Front, type/dia., in. ....Vented discs/13.0
Rear, type/dia., in. ....Vented discs/13.0
Anti-lock ....Not offered
Wheels and tires
Wheel size, in. ....17 x 10.0/17 x 13.0
Wheel type/material ....Cast aluminum
Tire size 275/40ZR17/335/35ZR17
Tire mfr. and model ....Michelin XGT Z

INSTRUMENTATION
Instruments ....180-mph speedo; 7000-rpm tach; oil pressure; fuel level; coolant temp; battery; digital clock
Warning lamps ....Check engine

PERFORMANCE AND TEST DATA
Acceleration, sec
  0-30 mph 2.1
  0-40 mph 2.8
  0-50 mph 3.6
  0-60 mph 4.7
  0-70 mph 5.9
  0-80 mph 7.7
Standing quarter mile
  sec @ mph ....13.1 @ 108.8
Braking, ft
  60-0 mph 145
Handling
  Lateral acceleration, g 0.97
  Speed through 600-ft
    slalom, mph 68.4
Speedometer error, mph
  Indicated   Actual
    30..32
    40..42
    50..52
    60..62

Interior noise, dBA
  Idling in neutral 70
  Steady 60 mph in top gear 81

FUEL ECONOMY
EPA, mpg 13/22
Est. range city/hwy., miles 286/484

Chrysler's second coming

America's third giant is back from the brink and casting an eye at the UK. Bob Murray reports from the US

THE CHRYSLER TECHnician leaning on the railings watching the Viper circulate had words for one Viper driver only, and it wasn't any of the UK motoring press corps. "When you see the way Bob Lutz comes through here, two wheels almost in the dirt, and then turns through that fast corner, well, man, that's *really* something." No surprise that Lutz holds the unofficial lap record around the Chrysler handling track in the V10 Viper; no surprise, either, that Lutz's regular job is president of the company. Lutz is like that. Chrysler in 1992 is like that. Call it gung-ho.

Chrysler? We're not talking about Hillman Avengers and Talbot Horizons but Chrysler Corp of Detroit, Michigan. Lee Iacocca's company, the company that owns Lamborghini.

The third of the big three US car makers, very nearly the first to hand in its chips and, since getting out of Rootes, the only one of the three without a mainstream European division. The first US manufacturer to bite the bullet to cut costs and reorganise itself out of the traditional US car-making norm. The company that has Bob Lutz, car nut and former Ford Europe driving force, and the company that now has Bob Eaton, engineer of both cars and GM Europe's latter-day success, ready to take over as chairman when Iacocca retires at the end of the year.

Chrysler still has a long way to go — including, from 1993, across the Atlantic into the UK — but no one doubts it is back. With new people, a new technical centre, a new way of working and new cars such as the extraordinary Viper and the Range Rover-rivalling Jeep Grand Cherokee, it is also back with a flair that a few years ago would have been hard to imagine. Chrysler's second coming.

Looking at the Viper helps you to understand Chrysler today. This is no hardship, for here is a sensational

Viper is more than an image boost, as this USA Today cutting shows

Viper and Cherokee cop car laid on for UK press corps

sports car, as spectacular to look at and drive as it is important for what it represents.

The Viper has four fathers: Lutz, design chief Tom Gale, engineering chief Francois Castaing and Carroll Shelby, the man who mixed British sports car with American muscle to create the '60s AC Cobra, the one car the Viper seeks most to emulate. So it's a back-to-basics sports car, which in the American way means a vast engine — an eight-litre V10 boasting no less than 400bhp and 450lb ft of torque — rear-wheel drive, massive tyre footprint, an open two-seat cabin and a body design that brings eyes out on stalks.

Part of new tech centre

And it goes as well as it ought: *Road & Track* magazine credits it with 0-60mph in 4.8secs and 0-100 in 11.1secs. Top speed is 160mph, which shows how tall the gearing and how awful the aerodynamics

Viper team all volunteers

are: the theoretical maximum is 300mph at the 6000rpm red line in sixth gear.

The Viper is surprisingly roomy for two. The driving position is good, it's easy and smooth to drive, goes like a train (and, unfortunately, the pushrod V10 rather sounds like one). On a smooth track, it has formidable grip with clean, quick responses for catchable tail slides when the thundering mid-range grunt overwhelms even the traction of the 335/35 ZR17 gumboots at the back. It's a shame about the noisy, blustery cabin and the ugly, Morgan-like detachable side screens. Still, the Viper by Chrysler, its British name, is an honest-to-goodness, high-power sports car that doesn't pretend to be anything else. I defy any enthusiasts to say they don't want one.

Chrysler needs it, and not just for the image boost. The Viper is an excellent example of that most challenging of products for a mass car maker outside Japan: a niche model.

Chrysler's way of doing it is to set up a small, select team and let it get on with the job well outside the corporate system. The Viper team wields a spanner or makes the coffee as necessary.

A Viper starts life as a collection of parts supplied by both Chrysler (the pushrod alloy V10 engine, and some suspension components) and a raft of outside suppliers, including ones for the tubular steel chassis and ready-painted plastic body. All the people at Mack Avenue have to do is put everything together. This is easier than it might sound because all Vipers are to the same specification.

Mack Avenue is not an impressive place, although there can be no doubt about the quality of the car or

> "There can be no doubting the quality of the car or the team's efficiency"

has just finished the 200th, with the first examples hitting US roads, in the hands of some big-name owners, about now. The first full year of production, next year, is said to be sold out — maximum capacity is 5000 a year. The British importer wants 50 cars and one will be shown at Birmingham in October, but it remains to be seen how many will make it here in 1993. A guide price is about £50,000, which is disappointing given that the car sells in the US for $50,000 and will only ever be available as a left-hooker.

As a sexy sports car, the Viper is useful to Chrysler but the way it was developed may yet prove crucial. The question is: how do you establish the same efficient, fast, dedicated team when the car is to be made in facility to make it happen is more than just hot air. This is Chrysler's new $1 billion Technology Centre, where design, engineering, manufacturing and supply are put together under one vast roof so completely that a new car can be taken from a drawing to driveable prototype without having to leave the complex.

The new LH cars just launched in the US — big four-door saloons called Chrysler Concorde, Eagle Vision and Dodge Intrepid — were the first to be influenced by this approach. Chrysler's first new saloon platform for 11 years is a bold venture at a time when new models are desperately needed and is one of the reasons why, at the end of July, Chrysler posted interim profits twice as good as expected.

Eight-litre V10 — 400bhp worth — is installed by hand

Murray sets off for Viper laps; car is cinch to drive well

— just 39 craftsmen and seven managers — has set up shop in the corner of an old warehouse in Mack Avenue, Detroit. All are volunteers with an average of 20 years at Chrysler — the *creme de la creme*. There are no supervisors, no hierarchy: everyone the enthusiasm and efficiency of the Detroit team. The Viper plant is an object lesson in how a large manufacturer can come up with small-selling but high-profile cars both quickly and efficiently.

The Viper team is currently making two cars a day and ▶ the hundreds of thousands a year rather than just 5000? Chrysler's "breakthrough" with what it calls platform teams may be just a new way of describing simultaneous engineering, where design and manufacturing work together from stage one, but the new

The other thing that has helped the company's balance sheet is increasing US demand for its two old stagers, the Jeep Cherokee four-wheel drive and the hugely successful Voyager MPV. The Cherokee, which was inherited from AMC when Chrysler bought it in 1987, is the advance party of Chrysler's return to the UK, paving the way for the new Grand Cherokee and a new version of the Voyager, with right-hand drive, from 1996.

Quite how far Chrysler's international ambitions extend is not yet known; that it has the people and facilities to produce cars that can compete worldwide cannot be doubted. Neither can the fact that first it has to succeed in the US. For a hometown boy without any important overseas relatives, achieving that *and* building cars for Europe will be a tough assignment, however gung-ho it may be. ■

Viper cabin notable for room, comfort and good quality

Dodge's favourite decades

DODGE VIPER

PHOTO BY JOHN LAMM

Three years ago, Chrysler announced it would build a 2-seat minimalist sports car on the order of the 427 Cobra. It seemed too good to be true, especially the part about it having a 400-bhp V-10 engine. What car company in its right mind would create such a thing? It might make a good show car, but surely it will never reach production, right?

Wrong. By March of 1992, you'll be able to walk into your local Dodge store and drive home what seems like a fantasy, a Dodge Viper. Why would Chrysler build it? For the same reason Chevrolet builds Corvettes: They don't do a lot for the company's bottom line, but they improve the image. Chrysler needs an image booster, a car that draws attention to itself and to the coming new Chrysler products that will either make or break the company before the end of the decade.

Though the Viper was built with an eye on the future, it smacks of the past. As everyone knows by now, Carroll Shelby had a part in the Viper project—though no one is saying how large a part—and the Viper's vital statistics are similar to the Cobra's. Like Shelby's sports car, the Chrysler has a steel tube frame with A-arms and coil springs at all four corners and a huge, normally aspirated engine up front. Steering is by rack-and-pinion.

But here's where similarities end. The Viper has ten holes where the Cobra had only eight. And while the engine is based on an upcoming Chrysler truck engine, its block is aluminum and is said to be very different from its parent. Lamborghini did the original castings for the Viper engine, but production cars will have engines made and assembled in the U.S. The transmission will be a 6-speed manual, a Borg-Warner unit, not the expected Getrag.

While the Cobra had a skin of alloy, the Viper's body will be a new type of glass-reinforced plastic. Viper components will come together in the company's New Mack assembly plant in Detroit. Virtually handbuilt, the cars will be produced in low quantity by domestic-car standards. For 1992, Chrysler plans to build between 200 and 500. The assembly process could produce as many as 5000 Vipers per year, but Chrysler says it expects to make about 1000 annually, or as many as the market demands. Low production almost always means high price, and the Viper is no exception. The good news is, the latest estimates put the price at $50,000—$10,000 less than was originally expected.

If you still won't believe it until you see it, the Viper's official launch takes place in January at the International Auto Show in Detroit.

SPECIFICATIONS

Base price, base model	est $50,000	
Country of origin	U.S.A.	
Body/seats	conv/2	
Layout	F/R	
Wheelbase	96.2 in.	
Track, f/r	59.6 in./60.8 in.	
Length	172.0 in.	
Width	75.6 in.	
Height	46.2 in.	
Luggage capacity	na	
Curb weight	2990 lb	
Fuel capacity	na	
Fuel economy (EPA):		
City	na	
Highway	na	
Engine	400-bhp ohv V-10	
Bore x stroke	101.6 x 98.6 mm	
Displacement	7989 cc	
Compression ratio	na	
Horsepower, SAE net	400 bhp @ 5500 rpm	
Torque	450 lb-ft @ 2200 rpm	
Transmission	6M	
Suspension, f/r	Ind/Ind	
Brakes, f/r	disc/disc	
Tires	275/40ZR-17f, 335/35ZR-17r	
Steering type	rack & pinion	
Turning circle	38.4 ft	
Warranty, years/miles:		
Bumper-to-bumper	1/12,000[1]	
Powertrain	7/70,000[1]	
Rust-through	7/100,000	
Driver's side passive restraint	motorized belt	

*indicates model described in specifications; na means information is not available.
[1] Combined 3/36,000 bumper-to-bumper and powertrain warranty optional at no extra cost.

PREVIEW TEST **CAR AND DRIVER**

Dodge Viper RT/10

Scoop: We become the first on earth to measure
the speed of the Viper's strike.

BY KEVIN SMITH

PHOTOGRAPHY BY RICK CASEMORE

The windows don't roll up. Matter of fact, there are no windows. Or outside door handles. Not much protection against the weather, either—the "top" is simply a section of canvas that stretches from the windshield header to the "sport bar." There is no hard top.

But what there is in this Dodge Viper RT/10 is a ten-cylinder, 488-cubic-inch powerplant producing 400 horsepower and a *Car and Driver*–measured 13.2-second quarter-mile time that makes it quicker than the altogether outrageous Chevrolet Corvette ZR-1.

And with the wind ripping new configurations in your eyebrows and the engine in full honk, you're not going to give one whit about absent windows or door handles. Because this Viper is one of the most exciting rides since Ben Hur discovered the chariot.

That's the whole point of the Viper. It's intended to go fast, stop hard, hang onto corners, and give everyone in sight—driver, passenger, and bystanders—a thrill that will make their day.

The Viper's massive ten-cylinder engine is mated to a six-speed transmission. An arresting plastic body hides a stout, steel-tube frame. There's also an unequal-length control-arm suspension, giant disc brakes, and wider-than-wide tires and wheels. And the entire exotic

package weighs in at 3450 pounds, ready to rumble.

For about $55,000, you too can hop inside. Getting in begins with an awkward reach inside and a tug of the too-conventional Chrysler-style door handle, and the door opens. (An aside: your government says car doors need locks and would not grant the Viper an exemption, creating the curious circumstance of inside door locks that are readily accessible from the outside.) Lowering yourself into the cockpit is easier than dropping into a Corvette—which has taller rocker structures—but you must heed the label warning of doorsill heat from the enclosed side exhausts. Once settled in the supportive, leather-faced bucket seat, the view that greets you is at once unusual (white-faced instru-

ments in an unappealing gray panel material that looks and feels like double-ought sandpaper) and welcoming (familiar, straightforward controls and switches).

At first, you think the clutch feels oddly unyielding, but that's the brake; the pedals are offset to the left because of that great honking front-mounted motor squeezing its way into the passenger compartment.

Not even the most jaded long-time owner will ever reach for the Viper's ignition switch without a palpable twinge of excitement. Lighting off ten 799cc cylinders will always arouse the spirit. The sound that follows, unfortunately, doesn't. Good mechanical busyness and a hungry-mouth intake roar comes from the front, but the separate, five-cylinder, side-outlet exhaust plumbing gave the engineers fits. They couldn't tune in a melodious note *and* meet the federal 80-dBA noise limit. So the Viper sounds oddly like a UPS truck up to 3000 rpm, then it just roars like God's own Dustbuster.

Pulling out into city traffic for the first time is less intimidating than it might be in a car like this. The clutch action is moderately heavy but smooth in takeup, the shift lever moves with unexpected ease, and—noise aside—the engine doesn't seem to care if it's turning 1200 or 5000 rpm. It always offers great thrust and never bucks or spits or overheats. The steering effort is light, and the brake pedal has absolutely no lost motion. In short, despite its Hulk Hogan presence, the Viper is a pussycat to drive. Its standard six-speaker stereo even works acceptably, with just a bit of musical detail lost to three-digit wind speeds. One feature we miss is a good left-foot dead pedal.

We found the Viper oddly difficult to see out of—a strange complaint in an open car. The windshield frame is quite thick, close by the driver's eyes, and low on top. We were continually ducking down to spot

road signs and traffic lights, and finally just slid down and forward in the seat to lower our vantage point. The sport bar behind the headrests also cut off the top of the inside mirror's view.

The Viper tolerates the urban crush, but it lives and breathes on open roads. Be they fast or slow, it pounds along happily. It does prefer smooth surfaces, since its radically wide tires display the usual big-meat tendency to juke about trying to follow contours and ripples in the pavement. At elevated speeds and cornering loads, this action can be startling; a sharp bump in the middle of a high-g turn is bad enough if it causes momentary unweighting of the tires, but in the Viper that event can be accompanied by a sharp lateral feint. Even traveling straight, a big, suspension-pumping undulation in the road

can threaten to change heading.

That was the closest thing to a disconcerting trait we found. During our test drive on California Route 33's fast sweeping turns north of Ojai, the big car felt solid, secure, and predictable for the most part. It is nicely balanced, with a little polite understeer most of the time, and the Michelin XGT-Zs' breakaway is not particularly sudden. Aside from initial steering response that at first seems a bit abrupt, there is no trick to making this car do what you want. It even rides well, with minimal harshness and a sense of tremendous structural rigidity.

Which is not to pretend that no one will ever fall behind a Viper and be bitten. The engine makes so much power and the tires generate so much grip that the car can

work up tremendous speed without sweat or drama, and *that* could prove deceptive. High limits, once they're exceeded, mean big trouble.

Yet isn't that much of the appeal? Not the danger itself, but the awesome potential, the no-foolin' manner—those same qualities that demand respect also make a machine like this irresistible. It worked for the original Cobra, it still motivates lots of Cobra-replica buyers, and now it is firing enthusiasm for a wild new big-engined sports roadster from a highly unlikely source.

In the process—and this may be the great payoff—the landmark Dodge Viper RT/10 has brought a new word into the modern lexicon of automotive passion: "Chrysler." •

Vehicle type: front-engine, rear-wheel-drive, 2-passenger, 2-door roadster

Estimated price as tested: $54,640

Estimated price and option breakdown: base Dodge Viper RT/10 (includes $1700 gas-guzzler tax, $700 freight, and $2240 luxury tax), $54,640

Major standard accessories: power steering, tilt steering

Sound system: Chrysler/Alpine AM/FM-stereo radio/cassette, 6 speakers

ENGINE
Type ....V-10, aluminum block and heads
Bore x stroke......................4.00 x 3.88 in, 101.6 x 98.6mm
Displacement ....488 cu in, 7990cc
Compression ratio.......................................9.1:1
Engine-control system........Chrysler with port fuel injection
Emissions controls ....3-way catalytic converter, feedback fuel-air-ratio control
Valve gear ....pushrods, hydraulic lifters
Power (SAE net) ....400 bhp @ 4600 rpm
Torque (SAE net) ....450 lb-ft @ 3600 rpm
Redline...6000 rpm

DRIVETRAIN
Transmission 6-speed
Final-drive ratio.....................................3.07:1, limited slip

Gear	Ratio	Mph/1000 rpm	Max. test speed
I	2.66	9.2	55 mph (6000 rpm)
II	1.78	13.8	83 mph (6000 rpm)
III	1.30	18.9	113 mph (6000 rpm)
IV	1.00	24.5	147 mph (6000 rpm)
V	0.74	33.2	159 mph (4800 rpm)
VI	0.50	49.0	120 mph (2450 rpm)

DIMENSIONS AND CAPACITIES
Wheelbase ....96.2 in
Track, F/R...59.6/60.8 in
Length ....175.1 in
Width ....75.7 in
Height...44.0 in
Curb weight ....3450 lb
Weight distribution, F/R 50/50%
Fuel capacity ....22.0 gal
Oil capacity ....11.0 qt
Water capacity ....14.0 qt

CHASSIS/BODY
Type..........................steel tubing frame integral with body
Body material ....fiberglass-reinforced plastic

INTERIOR
SAE volume, front seat..48 cu ft
         luggage space ....12 cu ft
Front seats ....bucket
Restraint systems ....door-mounted 3-point belts

SUSPENSION
F: ....ind, unequal-length control arms, coil springs, anti-roll bar
R: ....ind, unequal-length control arms with a toe-control link, coil springs, anti-roll bar

STEERING
Type ....rack-and-pinion, power-assisted
Turns lock-to-lock 2.4
Turning circle curb-to-curb ....40.7 ft

BRAKES
F: ....13.0 x 1.3-in vented disc
R: ....13.0 x 0.9-in vented disc
Power assist ....vacuum

WHEELS AND TIRES
Wheel size ....F: 10.0 x 17 in, R: 13.0 x 17 in
Wheel type ....cast aluminum hub, spun aluminum rim
Tires ....Michelin XGT-Z, F: P275/40ZR-17, R: P335/35ZR-17
Test inflation pressures, F/R................................35/35 psi

CAR AND DRIVER TEST RESULTS

ACCELERATION — Seconds
Zero to 30 mph...1.8
         40 mph...2.5
         50 mph...3.7
         60 mph...4.6
         70 mph...5.7
         80 mph...7.6
         90 mph...9.1
        100 mph...11.7
        110 mph...14.0
        120 mph...16.6
Street start, 5–60 mph..4.9
Top-gear passing time, 30–50 mph ........................N.A.
                       50–70 mph........................10.6
Standing ¼-mile................................13.2 sec @ 107 mph

Top speed ....159 mph

BRAKING
70–0 mph @ impending lockup ....193 ft
Modulation ....poor fair **good** excellent
Fade ....**none** moderate heavy
Front-rear balance..................................poor **fair** good

HANDLING
Roadholding, 300-ft-dia skidpad.............................0.85 g
Understeer.....................**minimal** moderate excessive

PROJECTED FUEL ECONOMY
EPA city driving ....14 mpg
EPA highway driving ....19 mpg

STARS 'N' STRIPES

Generally, a show car like the Viper will get its photograph in a couple of dozen car magazines and newspapers, and maybe receive a 30-second shot on the evening TV news. That's about it. So, after making several thousand revolutions on its neon-lit turntable, and being leaned on by an assortment of Cosmopolitan-reject models, most show cars receive an unceremonious truck trip to the engineering building, where they're dismantled and dumped in the crusher.

That was not the fate of Viper. The car's stint on the motorshow in 1989 created a fervour. Near-riot conditions were occurring on a regular basis as seemingly normal showgoers pushed and shoved their fellow man just to get near the V-10-powered roadster. The most fortunate souls got close enough to snap a photo, or perhaps stretch out and touch a fender as it pirouetted by on the moving stage. But, the majority only glimpsed it between the bobbing heads of those in front, though even that was impetus enough to spring to action: to become an active part of the most intense grassroots letter writing campaign Chrysler had ever been deluged with.

Within a few weeks of the initial public display, Chrysler Chairman Lee Iacocca began receiving mailsacks crammed to capacity with cards and letters demanding that the Viper be built. By the time the enthusiastic magazine articles had hit the streets, Viper fever had reached boiling point. It was obvious: This was no flash in the pan. Viper was a 400hp (298 kW) goodwill campaign that brought more positive attention to Chrysler than a hundred million dollars' worth of advertising could buy.

THAT ONE HUNK OF STEEL and fibreglass, originally designed to have a six month shelf-life, had become the most important thing Chrysler had created since the minivan. And, being the artful promoter he's renowned for, Iaococca knew he had to do something to keep Viper fever alive. He had to bring the car to production.

So, now it's 1993. The Viper assembly line is in full swing, and a couple of hundred lucky buyers have plonked down their $US50,000+ for a chance at one of the second-year cars. But, the magazine articles and TV coverage for Viper have begun to wane. The company has invested millions to let the world know about the new LH series of sedans, and is advertising the Jeep Grand Cherokee on every billboard across America. Costly stuff, indeed. Therefore, what Chrysler needs now is another bunch of free publicity. Another round of Viper fever.

Which brings us to the Viper GTS Coupe. Another machine purpose-built for the car show circuit. Another Dodge that'll rip your head off with its looks. Another case of Viper fever.

This is a Viper designed for improved real-world use. It has a hardtop. It has roll-up side windows. It has scoops, spoilers, slats and stripes. It has an attitude that's twice as mean as the Viper RT/10 roadster, and a hundred-fold nastier than anything else built in America. Sculpted to maximise high speed stability, not for slippery wind tunnel C_d numbers, the Viper GTS is not what you'd call an aerodynamic breakthrough. Chrysler isn't releasing C_d numbers for the car (nor has it for the regular Viper) but we have it on good authority that the Viper roadster bucks the wind at about a 0.40 C_d. The more flamboyant GTS Coupe, however, may be more aero as well, due to the fact that cars with full roofs and closed windows are typically "cleaner" than their corresponding open-cockpit models.

At the front there's a lower, more pronounced facia to discourage airflow from under the car, and huge extractor grates on the tops of the front fenders to scavenge out air that'd normally pack up in the wheelwells at high speeds — which should improve high speed stability and

A 400 horsepower goodwill campaign... the Viper GTS is not lacking in what red-blooded Yankee buyers want: solid, big engine grunt from the 8.0-litre V10.

The cockpit of the Viper GTS is essentially the same as in the RT/10, though Tom Gale's designers have changed the view a bit by adding a flat-black dashboard covering and black gauges with white numerals (as opposed to the RT/10's white gauges with black numerals). Real six-point racing harnesses are used, but would not pass the US regulations for passive restraints, and could not be used in a production vehicle. There is no airbag, but development is underway for one.

Chrysler's vice president of product design, Tom Gale, was given the tough assignment of constructing a Viper hardtop to be even more head-turning than its roadster counterpart. He's succeeded.

may even increase top speed by a couple of km/h. As well, a ram-air induction system has been added simply by cutting a hole in the centre of the hood and installing a no-drag NACA duct, thereby force-feeding high speed oxygen (and some unlucky bugs) directly into the airbox.

THE HARDTOP IS WELL INTEGRATED into the Viper's original lines, and keeps the muscular character of the machine intact. Styling cues taken from the 1965 Shelby Cobra Daytona race car are evident all-around, but are most obvious at the rear of the car. The tie-in to Carroll Shelby's famous race machine did not happen by accident; Shelby is a consultant to Chrysler, and had a strong hand in the development of the Viper RT/10 (though less interaction with the GTS Coupe).

Most flattering when viewed from above, the roof structure utilises a large lift-up rear glass hatch and twin "blisters" in the roof panel to provide extra headroom inside — therefore allowing room for driver and passenger to wear helmets. A quick-fill gas cap has been added to the right-side B-pillar, and funnels high octane to a bladder-type fuel cell. The original trunk lid has been eliminated, and the back area of the car has been converted into a carpeted storage area accessible only through the glass hatch. Overall cargo space is slightly reduced compared with the RT/10, but its usefulness is improved, and there's now a full-size spare tyre.

Inner panels serve as air extractors from the wheelwells, and also aid high speed stability. A small spoiler has been added to the deck, and helps to finish off the Kammback look of the GTS with an incredibly aggressive attitude.

A pair of chromed exhaust tips poke out of the rear lower fascia, and deliver the improved tone of all 10 cylinders firing, as opposed to the standard Viper's operational side pipes that give you only the sound of an uneven five cylinders at your ear. The GTS show car also runs basically uncorked (no catalytic converters) and sounds much more nasty because of it. Surprisingly, the RT/10's standard-issue side pipes remain in place under the doors, but are now merely cosmetic trim items — looking embarrassingly out of character for this no-frills performance machine.

All other Vipers built so far have been bright red, which makes the sight of this deep blue beast with bright white racing stripes a real traffic-stopper. Compared with the regular production Viper, the GTS is about 113 kg heavier (at about 1585 kg) due to the hardtop components and glasswork. Since the same 400 bhp (298 kW), 8.0-litre, V-10 engine and six-speed manual transmission is used in both, the GTS Coupe can be expected to perform just a bit less awesomely than does the Viper RT/10. Remember, though, the regular Viper accelerates from 0-100 km/h in 4.9 seconds, does the quarter-mile in 13.10 sec/175 km/h, charges to nearly 270 km/h in top speed, and generates close to 1.0g in lateral grip.

Styling curves have been integrated into the rearmost edges of the back bumpers, improving the Viper's appearance.

So, even if it's a bit slower, the GTS would still be one of the quickest new cars on the street. The tyre/wheel size has not been changed from that of the RT/10, but there are delicious new chromed five-spoke 17-inch alloy wheels supporting the wide Michelin radials.

Anti-lock brakes will never be used on the minimalist-themed Viper (according to Chrysler's vice president of vehicle engineering, Francois Castaing) even though the computer-controlled binders would help shorten the car's high speed braking distances and improve inclement weather stoppability.

Chrysler has not decided to produce the GTS Coupe as of now, but is closely watching the American public's reaction at the auto shows this year. One would guess, however, that since Chrysler is undoubtedly looking to keep Viper fever alive into 1994 and beyond, that moving the GTS into production-ready status would be a smart idea. Besides, the car is 90 per cent of what a regular Viper is, and only needs the top structure and a few other cosmetic changes to make the transformation.

That doesn't seem like such a tough project, either from a financial or time-scheduling standpoint.

Come on, Chrysler, the time is right. M

DODGE VIPER GTS COUPE
8.0-litre, 6-sp man

Engine:	front, longitudinally-mounted, V10 electronic multi-point fuel injection
Valve gear:	push-rod operated ohv, two valves/cyl
Power:	298 kW @ 4600 rpm
Torque:	609 Nm @ 3600 rpm
Front suspension:	Independent by double wishbones, adjustable dampers, coil springs and anti-roll bar
Rear suspension:	Double wishbones, separate toe link, adjustable dampers, anti-roll bar
Price:	n/a
Likes:	wild styling, wild performance
Dislikes:	Rear view blind spot over driver's shoulder

Viper vs. Corvette ZR-1

There are no other cars quite like the Dodge Viper RT/10, but one obvious standard for comparison is Chevrolet's Corvette ZR-1, the reigning king of American speedsters and one of the fastest cars anywhere. Though open-car aerodynamics will keep the ZR-1's 170-plus-mph top speed safe, the Viper seems otherwise competitive. It weighs 69 pounds less than the last ZR-1 we tested (April 1991), and the big V-10 engine holds an advantage in both horsepower (400 at 4600 rpm versus 375 at 5800) and torque (450 pound-feet at 3600 rpm versus 370 at 5600). The Viper pulls even taller gearing—barely 1300 rpm at 65 mph in sixth and too tall to execute our 30-to-50-mph top-gear acceleration test—than the long-legged Corvette, with 3.07:1 final drive compared with the Corvette's 3.45. Ratios inside the two six-speed gearboxes are, coincidentally, almost identical.

Both transmissions offer the funky first-to-fourth "skip shift" feature in grudging deference to the EPA—though the Viper's operates in such a narrow speed range that it rarely intruded on our driving. Unlike the Corvette engineers, Team Viper did not have to avoid the gas-guzzler penalty. The ZR-1's 16/25 EPA mileage figures beat the Viper's 14/19 projections.

Massive seventeen-inch tires and wheels support both cars, but the Viper claims an edge in footprint with its 335/35 rear tires on thirteen-inch rims. The Corvette's are 315/35s on eleven-inchers. All else being equal (which it rarely is), more rubber and less weight should mean greater cornering grip. And the Viper's advantage in brake swept area—519 square inches to 422—should translate to superior braking. The Viper, however, does without the complexity of ABS—and of traction control, adjustable damping, and a driver's air bag, all standard on the ZR-1.

In the dollar derby, the Viper's relative simplicity seems to pay off. It carries a $54,640 estimated price tag, whereas the ZR-1 lists for $69,455. Early Viper buyers will likely pay a premium, however, while ZR-1s are currently being discounted.

Clandestine and admittedly incomplete instrumented testing of our Viper photo car lets us confirm some of Chrysler's performance claims and assess how the Viper stacks up against the ZR-1. We ran to a true 159 mph, with a smidgeon more to come. Chrysler lists a top speed of 165—probably in reach under ideal conditions. Our last ZR-1 went 171 mph. Advantage, Chevrolet.

This Viper's 0-to-60 time of 4.6 seconds backs up Chrysler's quoted 4.5 and edges the ZR-1's 4.9. In 0-to-100, however, aerodynamics and multivalve breathing start to tell, and the ZR-1 pulls ahead, 11.3 seconds to 11.7. The quarter-mile is almost even, the Viper posting a 13.2-second, 107-mph run, the ZR-1 13.4 seconds at 109 mph.

Chrysler touts the Viper's ability to do 0 to 100 to 0 (accelerate to 100 from a standing start then brake to a stop) in 14.5 seconds. We've never measured that "test," but our Viper needed all but 2.8 of those 14.5 seconds to reach 100, so we're skeptical, especially in light of a rather average 70-to-0 stopping distance: 193 feet, against the ZR-1's 159.

Was our pre-production Viper completely healthy, performing as sharply as final production examples will? Perhaps not. But, in any case, nuances of suspension geometry, balance, and control response can play almost as big a role in measured performance as the on-paper basics of mass, power, and footprint. We only had the chance to run the Viper on a wet skidpad, where it generated 0.85 g, so beating the ZR-1's 0.87 g is quite likely.

Clearly, the Viper RT/10 deserves to be mentioned along with the Corvette ZR-1 in any discussion of America's great performers. But the King doesn't look ready to relinquish his crown just yet. —*KS*

SECOND STRIKE

First, Dodge created the Viper—the Shelby Cobra for the Nineties. Now it has built the Viper cou-

show car inspired by the Cobra Daytona competition model. What's next, an assault on Le Mans?

Auburn Hills, Michigan—

The message is the war paint. Bold white racing stripes draped over gleaming ocean-blue pearlescent bodywork, a combination straight out of the 1960s—the competition livery, in fact, of the Shelby American Cobra Daytona competition coupes that beat Ferrari for the 1965 World Manufacturers' Championship for Grand Touring cars. On most of today's automobiles, a paint scheme like this would look ludicrous, but on the Viper GTS coupe, Dodge's new one-off show car, it's perfect. Nothing could better

BY RICH CEPPOS

PHOTOGRAPHY BY MICHAEL GASPAR

VIPER COUPE

express the visceral connection between the Viper coupe and the legendary racing Cobra of twenty-eight years ago.

Although the Viper GTS looks like it is descended directly from the Cobra Daytona coupe, that simple observation does not explain its true purpose. Is it a pre-production version of a new model we will soon be able to buy? Is it, like the Cobra Daytona, destined to be one of a handful of competition cars built exclusively for the factory to race? Or is Dodge sending it out on the auto-show circuit simply to tease us until we weep?

We asked Neil Walling, Chrysler's director of advanced and international design—the man in charge of this project. "I'd be lying if I said to you the Cobra Daytona coupe isn't part of the inspiration for the GTS. But this is *not* a production car. Right now we have no plans to produce this car at all."

The project was commissioned, he explains, "to test the market, much like we did with the original Viper show car—to see if there's interest out there. And we do want to keep people talking about the Viper. There are a lot of things

Genesis of a show car: The Cobra Daytona competition coupe, above, was piloted by such luminaries as Dan Gurney, Phil Hill, Bob Bondurant, and Maurice Trintignant. It inspired the Viper coupe drawings that showed up in a photo of Tom Gale in our June 1992 issue. Right, the highly detailed three-eighths-scale wind-tunnel model.

SHOP PHOTOS BY KEN OSBURN

Assembly took place off Chrysler property in a top-secret shop in a Detroit suburb. Every one of the Viper roadster's body panels was modified in some way; the coupe's doors contain roll-up windows (the roadster has no side glass).

you could do with the coupe." Walling is grinning now. "You could put it into production, or you could build a dozen or so and campaign them. But before you do anything like that, you have to do the first one."

The first one, explains Walling, "came as much as anything from designers saying 'wouldn't it be neat if...'" Walling recalls Chrysler design chief Tom Gale asking what a competition Viper coupe or roadster would look like, "and after that a designer does a sketch, and more and more people say, 'Gee, that would be neat.' It's an important part of creativity that we try to foster in allowing our people to have fun with their work—allowing people to pursue things that intuitively seem exciting and interesting. If you try to format all the design work, then suddenly everything gets distilled down to a neutral shade of gray."

There is more to the Viper GTS, however, than just the designers' gut-level instincts about what a car like this should look like: There is science. A detailed three-eighths-scale clay model was developed during the design process for extensive wind tunnel tests. "We thought of the GTS in terms of what you'd want if you were running it in competition," says Walling.

The wind tunnel work resulted in modifications to the front air dam, the addition of a pair of serious-looking vents atop the front fenders to relieve pressure from within the fender wells, a NACA duct in the hood for more efficient airflow to the engine, and a ducktail rear spoiler that adds downforce. Walling says, "We achieved neutral lift

front-to-rear,'' which is a vast improvement over the Viper roadster. The need to improve the aerodynamics of the original Cobra roadster, by the way, was the sole reason the Daytona coupe was built; the roadster suffered from too much aerodynamic drag to be competitive with Ferrari's GTOs on high-speed European road courses like Le Mans.

It seems odd that Dodge would invest time and money improving the aerodynamics of a show car it has no plans to build. ''Well, you do have to do your homework,'' says Walling. ''When you show a car to the public, you're committed. You don't want to show it and then, if it goes into production, have to make a lot of changes to it because certain things aren't feasible.'' We'll take that as a clear signal that Dodge hasn't ruled out production after all.

Exactly what a production Viper coupe would be like to live with is something we can only speculate about, even though we did climb behind the GTS's wheel and take it for a spin around the block. Our encounter came at the Chrysler Technology Center just after the car was finished, and scant hours before it was to roll onto a truck for the cross-country trek to the Los Angeles Auto Show.

Chrysler's design staff was understandably concerned about the well-being of its only Viper coupe, which took three-and-a-half months to hand-make (the paint job alone required sixty hours). One stone chip would have had half-a-dozen fabricators jumping from tenth-story windows, so we trundled around at low speed just to get a sense of the car.

Underneath the new GTS bodywork is stock Viper running gear. Compared with a Viper roadster, the only difference we found during our short ride—aside from the absence of wind in the cabin—was a wonderfully raw, Gatling-gun exhaust note that bellowed from the specially fabricated pipes that exit at the rear of the car. Finally, a Viper that sounded sufficiently bellicose—just like Cobras immemorial. Too bad Dodge can't make them all this way.

Whatever course the GTS project takes from here on, the man who designed the original Cobra Daytona coupe is flattered by the attention the special Viper focuses on his twenty-eight-year-old handiwork. Pete Brock, now in his fifties, came to Shelby American and penned the Daytona after a stint as a GM designer. The Cobra racing coupe was built directly from Brock's intuitive freehand sketches; no blueprints were ever drawn, nor were any wind tunnel tests ever conducted. "We did that project off in the corner because only a few of us at the shop really understood anything about high-speed European racetracks." Brock's design worked so well that the Cobra's top speed leapt from about 160 mph to more than 180. Six Daytona coupes were built in all.

"Tom Gale came by and showed me the initial drawings of the Viper coupe," says Brock, "and he asked if I minded them doing it that way, with the paint and all. Did I mind? I was honored. Just the fact that they would share what they were doing was extremely considerate of them."

And what does Mr. Brock think of the new coupe? He likes it. "I think the concept they've come up with on the coupe better reflects what the Cobra Daytona is than the Viper roadster reflects what the original Cobra is. The coupe is a lot more in keeping with the theme they were looking for."

We can only add that we hope the rest of the world finds ocean-blue Viper coupes with broad white stripes as captivating as we do. The power of public opinion made the Viper roadster a reality; it might just cause something magical to happen all over again.

The Viper coupe's 1960s race-car design theme is underscored by touches like a Le Mans flip-up fuel door and a full-size spare tire sitting exposed under the hatch glass. (The FIA rules for mid-1960s GT cars required the Cobra Daytonas to carry a spare in the same location.) The GTS's engine is a stock 400-bhp Viper V-10, which exhales through special low-restriction pipes that exit at the rear of the car.

DODGE VIPER GTS
Front-engine, rear-wheel-drive coupe
2-passenger, 2-door fiberglass body

POWERTRAIN:
OHV V-10, 488 cu in (7997 cc)
Power SAE net 400 bhp @ 5200 rpm
Torque SAE net 450 lb-ft @ 3600 rpm
6-speed manual transmission

CHASSIS:
Independent front and rear suspension
Power-assisted rack-and-pinion steering
Vented front and rear disc brakes
275/40ZR-17 front, 335/35ZR-17 rear Michelin tires

MEASUREMENTS:
Wheelbase 96.2 in
Length x width x height 175.1 x 75.7 x 44.0 in

Carroll Shelby's 427 Cobra was the inspiration for the Dodge Viper, so it is only logical that the car you see here, the Viper GTS coupe, should also draw heavily on Cobra history.

Dodge makes no apologies for it. "Where the Viper follows the classic sports car gospel [two seats and an open top], this time we looked at some of the great grand touring cars such as the Cobra Daytona Coupe and the Ferrari GTO," explains Francois Castaing, vice-president of engineering at parent company Chrysler.

The designer of the original Cobra Daytona, Peter Brock, reckons the Viper GTS would outsell its roadster sibling. If, that is, Chrysler were to put it into production.

It wouldn't be a particularly difficult project. The coupe is based very closely on the roadster, underpinned with its tubular steel chassis and graced with an exciting new body drawn up at Chrysler Design in Detroit. While the bonnet and door skins are taken from the roadster, the rest is new. At the front is a deep new air dam — probably too deep for production. Like the roadster, engine heat escapes through vents at the trailing edges of the front wings, but a NACA duct has been added on the front of the steeply sloping bonnet to feed cool air into the engine. On top of each front wing is a large louvre that lets air escape from underneath, reducing lift.

The roof of the coupe features a pair of bumps that are designed to increase headroom for helmeted drivers. The curvy shape, which has been tested in a wind tunnel to confirm its stability at all speeds and attitudes, then tapers rearward via a hinged, all-glass liftback to a tall duck-tail spoiler. The effect is stunning; the coupe is an immensely powerful-looking car, a machine with great presence and character.

"The design is somewhat analogous to a recipe," says Chrysler design chief Tom Gale. "I see a little bit of Ferrari 250 GTO and a heavy sprinkling of Peter Brock's Cobra Daytona Coupe — at least, that's what was in the back of our minds."

At one point Chrysler planned to call this car the Viper Daytona Coupe, but the feeling was that it might cause

Mean streak

As if the roadster wasn't enough, Dodge has uncoiled a truly mean Viper coupe. John Lamm reports

confusion with the production Dodge Daytona.

Chrysler president Bob Lutz adds: "To me, the Pete Brock Cobras were always one of the most fascinating — they were aerodynamic yet looked brutal, they radiated raw power, they were beautiful, they were American, they were all the right stuff. That's what we tried to recapture."

And they've succeeded, from the dark metallic blue paint with two wide white stripes (the same basic design as on the Daytona coupe) to the new, polished aluminium road wheels. Inside, the matt black instrument panel, the steering wheel and controls are those of the production Viper. New to the GTS are the seats, manually operated windows, five-point competition seat harnesses and fire extinguisher. A large competition-style fuel filler allows petrol to be dumped into a huge 35-gallon tank in the car's tail.

The GTS packs a standard Viper drivetrain: an eight-litre V10 developed by Lamborghini and good for 400bhp and 465lb ft of torque. The side exhaust pipes have been blanked off in favour of an 'export' exhaust system that runs to the rear of the car. Castaing points out that the GTS has no silencers: "It's pretty noisy — just the way it should be." The six-speed manual gearbox stays, as do the four-wheel independent suspension and four-wheel disc brakes (without anti-lock).

At 4516mm (177.8ins) long, the GTS is 69mm longer than the roadster, and the coupe body gains 119mm in height to 1237mm (48.7ins). The roof also adds weight.

"If we were to use the same plastics and the same RTM technology [as the roadster], we'd be adding something like 250lb [113kg] to make the coupe because it has more glass and other components," says Castaing. "A case can be made for changing the technology of the skin and keeping the car to the same weight. This is something we'll have to resolve, but if we were to keep it simple this car would be slower than the Viper, at least in cornering."

A programme is under way to shed weight from the Viper roadster to a target of 1360kg (3000lb), and those changes would be integrated into the GTS coupe.

On the coupe's potential top speed, Bob Lutz says:

IT'S GOT THE LOOK

Peter Brock, designer of the Cobra Daytona, assesses the car it inspired

Cobra Daytona Coupe was controversial in '60s

"IT'S A PRETTY HOT-LOOKING PIECE," PETER BROCK EXCLAIMS as we approach the Viper GTS. Chrysler's design chief, Tom Gale, had given Brock a sneak preview of the GTS sketches a few months before at the Monterey Historic Auto Races, but this was first time Brock had seen the car in the flesh. And his opinion counts because, as a young man working for Carroll Shelby in the '60s, he penned the shape of the Cobra Daytona Coupe.

When Gale asked him what he thought about Chrysler's GTS project, Brock was enthusiastic, recognising it as a tribute to the Daytona concept. "I think it's come off far more successfully as a coupe than it did as a roadster," he says.

"It's spectacular. It's big. I think the proportioning of the roof to the rest of the car makes the GTS look a little bit smaller, whereas the Viper tends to look overly large. By putting a roof on the Viper, I think it ties the thing together a little bit better.

"The windscreen design works very well and rounds the Viper coupe off. One of the real faults of the Daytona is that we couldn't run that type of [laid-back] screen or we would have been way forward over the engine airbox. I also think that if you set the GTS alongside the Daytona you'd find the Cobra is a really tiny car… almost the size of an Austin Healey Sprite. If you looked at the photographs of the two cars you wouldn't see the size difference, but if you put them side by side I think you'd notice there's a tremendous difference. So the GTS emulates the Daytona in form, but certainly not in size.

Brock: GTS 'spectacular'

"The thing that's really nice on this car," Brock adds, "and which mimics the Daytona, is that the roofline has the high spot over the driver's head. We didn't have the double bubble on ours, of course, but the GTS's high point is right where it should be, with the windscreen line much lower than the highest part of the roof. That was part of the controversy over the original Daytona. At that time it was considered very strange because in most contemporary coupes the high point was almost like an airfoil just a couple of inches behind the windscreen, and then they fastbacked off. So they tended to get a lot of lift. The Daytona had the high point over the driver with the whole roof slanting forward from that point, and it was a very strange-looking line."

For Brock, the GTS is a fine achievement in design terms. "It's not quite as 'boy racer' as the roadster, and I like that. I think things are a little more integrated and toned down on the coupe, and I like that too. I'm sure if Dodge decided to put the GTS on the market, they'd sell more of these than roadsters."

◀ "Obviously performance, especially the top end, is going to be way, way beyond that of the roadster because the GTS is aerodynamically a much better vehicle, so while we haven't done any calculations or tests, I would imagine that 200mph wouldn't be very far away."

Given the Cobra heritage of both Viper models, it's easy to picture them on the race track. Castaing, who as a young man saw the Daytonas compete at Le Mans, plays this down. "There has been speculation and discussion on whether the Viper should be a race car or not," he says. "Today, Chrysler and Dodge aren't very anxious to organise a Viper factory-sponsored racing effort because we feel the car has so much personality that racing it and adding spoilers and things like that wouldn't do much for its image. If people want to race the car, that's fine, but we won't be behind it."

Castaing, a one-time Renault F1 manager, adds that the issue has been further complicated by the imminent demise of Group C sportscar racing.

"FISA is still foundering on what they're going to do after killing Group C. There's some

All-glass liftback sweeps down to big duck-tail spoiler

Matt black facia carried over from Viper roadster

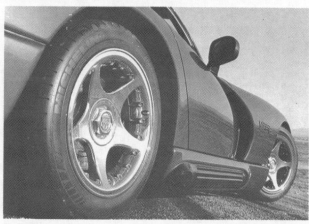
Polished aluminium wheels; side exhausts blanked off

discussion that it will be replaced by some kind of super-car racing. Obviously I'd love to see the racing flavour of the '60s come back, because those cars were terrific. I am not, however, sure that modern technology will make this dream feasible, because of the continuous technology race with electronics and things like that. But who knows?"

For that matter, who knows if the Viper GTS will ever be produced? Castaing says: "Some of us would like to make a car like the one here, kept simple and not a very complex offspring of the Viper. There are a few challenges, like the fact that this car is equipped with drop side window glass which forced us to remove the retractors for the seatbelts that we have in the doors, but we are planning to do that anyway to adapt airbags to the Viper.

"We had other new ideas on display at the Detroit show like the Plymouth Prowler street rod, and we don't know if we need to do more for Dodge right now. It may be, in the end, a tough choice of which project to do first.

"Maybe, if there is popular demand for it, we will be able to do everything."

Chrysler's UK arm is hoping to bring the car across the Atlantic, perhaps in time for the London Motor Show in October, to help swell this demand. But there are other elements in the equation, such as the critical matter of time, people and money. Chrysler has to choose where to concentrate its engineering resources, which aren't infinite.

"Chrysler isn't about to hire 1000 engineers, so we will have to make some tough choices between things like the electric van project, on-board diagnostic technologies and all the fun projects we feel we could keep doing," says Castaing. "Now that we have a way to test the market, which is to present the car at auto shows and ask the people if they would buy it, we'll do our best to satisfy everybody."

Lutz feels that there are well-to-do sports car *aficionados* who will want a Viper coupe as well as a roadster. "I'm certainly in that category. While the Viper turns everybody on, at some point people who live in rainy areas will start thinking about the practical aspects. With the coupe they could enjoy it all the time."

We certainly would. ■

Extra weight likely to affect handling, but improved aerodynamics will give higher top speed. Note 'double bubble' roof

New seats and harnesses

NACA duct feeds in air

Eight-litre V10 pumps out an earth-shattering 400bhp

Hennessey Venom 500 Viper

C. Van Tune sinks hyperbole-stained fangs into the torquemonster Hennessey Venom 500 Viper. Photographs by Scott Dahlquist and the author.

IMPRESSIONS

It ain't exactly like general science class, but play along with the metaphor anyway. Cars are animals. Or, at least, in a quasi-analytical sense, that's how we see them: thoroughbreds, tigers, dogs, pussycats, dinosaurs and so on. Maybe an occasional slug, for good measure.

Divided into more scientific terms, cars can also be classified in regard to their most basal attitudes: what they eat. Politically-correct, fuel-sipping, non-CFC-producing weenie machines like Honda Civics, Geo Prizms and every Volvo but the turbo models are the herbivores: meek, toast-eating, non-threatening cars for people who don't like to drive.

Next up are the omnivores, the more intelligent hunter/gatherers, wearing nameplates ranging from Audi to Saab and able to handily survive most roadside encounters. Pleasant enough to steer, but lacking the inner craving for fresh blood. These cars would just as soon have a salad as a lamb chop; they're hungry, but not ravenous.

Exterior (below) and interior (opposite, top) remain unchanged from stock. It's the engine (opposite, below) that comes in for serious changes in Hennessey's scheme. Power is up 100 bhp to 500 overall.

Then there are the carnivores. The T. rexes of jurassic torque. Ferrari 512TRs, Lamborghini Diablos, Porsche 911 Turbos, Dodge Vipers. Eternally seeking out the next victim to kill, to wholly disembowel as steam rises from the gaping wound. Badass cars. Cars so fast they frighten everyone, including the driver on occasion. Pretenders like the Corvette ZR-1 and Acura NSX try to belong in this coven, but don't pass the taste test—-way too civilized, preferring their meat cooked...oh, just so, please.

No thanks. Give me blood and guts anytime, preferably in the form of the Hennessey Motorsports Venom 500 Viper, a modified Mopar that's still as rough and caustic as the original but stuffed with an additional 100 horsepower. Output is 500 bhp at 5600 rpm, and 550 pound-feet of torque at 3800 rpm. It's a pissed-off brahma bull, a pit of rattlers, and a white-shark feeding frenzy wrapped into one. It'll hunt you down. It craves the kill.

▶ Snake Tech

Talk to a Team Viper engineer, and you'll quickly learn that the 8.0-liter pushrod V-10 is far from maxed out. Relying on mega-displacement to do its dirty work, this engine has plenty of untapped muscle in reserve. With a 6000-rpm redline and a torque band wide enough to resemble the Nebraska plains, here's one motor that begs for a serious hot-rod job.

The trick, quite simply, is to improve airflow, so the essence of Hennessey's Venom 500 system is far from complex. Included is cylinder-head porting, combustion-chamber shaping, valvetrain refinement, exhaust-system upgrading, a rear-gear change, and some minor software fiddling. Installed price for all the mods is $14,500, but they'll also sell most items separately to avoid an epidemic of shocked wallets and startled citizenry.

Heft open the clamshell hood, plant your fanny on one of the big front Michelins and prepare for the seminar, sonny. Beginning at the front of the motor, you'll find lower-restriction air filter elements that tuck away inside the stock airbox, allowing you to trash the cumbersome air filter resonators and improve the intake snarl. The inrushing air then finds its way past slightly enlarged (by 5mm) throttle bodies and into the hogged-out intake manifold. A full port-and-polish job improves airflow by about 30% and raises output by 20 horsepower. The stock fuel injectors are retained.

Eager to take part in the combustion process, the air hurries into the cylinder heads where the real magic occurs. Each head is ported, polished, port-matched to the intake manifold and tested on a SuperFlow airbench. A bit of machine work raises compression from 9.1 to 10.0:1, and roller rocker arms and new pushrods are dropped in place to reduce valvetrain friction. The resultant 30-35% increase in airflow equates to about 60 extra horsepower.

▶ Sound System

Okay, now the tough part. Fearsome levels of underhood muscle are just fine, but jeez, that exhaust note—*urban diaper-service trucks* sound more muscular. If it were *my* car, I'd rip the sidepipes off and run everything aft of the cats out the back end, like the Vipers destined for export duty will be outfitted. That way, your ears would hear a more symmetrical ten-cylinder tone from behind, not an uneven five at each side. Weld in a pair of Flowmasters—or just leave 'em as straight-pipes—and the improvement would be substantial.

But Hennessey's wrench-turners take a different approach. If the car's owner wants to retain the side pipes but create a better noise, larger 3.0-inch-diameter (up from 2.5-inch stock) pipes with high-flow (450 cfm) catalytic converters and Borla XR-1 mufflers are slid into place. A crossover tube is then fabricated and wrestled around the underbody confines to connect both exhaust banks, further enlivening the output note. Aural improvement by this

method is noticeable, but still far from the rasp of even a new Camaro Z28.

Having utilized most of the basic hot-rodding tricks short of nitrous injection or a cam change, Hennessey next concentrates on making the most of the engine's newfound power. The first thing to go is the factory-installed 3.07:1 ring and pinion, a super-tall economy and emissions gear

meant to please the feds, not the fanatics. Combined with the standard Borg-Warner T-56 gearbox and its 0.50:1 sixth-gear cogs, this ultra-overdrive setup lets you chug along at 100 mph while taching a lowly 2000 rpm. Sixth is simply too tall for any sort of performance driving, even with the mountainous torque of this engine.

The Dana rear end eagerly accepts deeper 3.73:1 gearing, which give the car its greatest single performance boost of all the items in Hennessey's repertoire. The engine swings more rapidly through its powerband in each gear, and highway revs go up by only a few hundred.

Except for the addition of any owner-mandated safety gear, the Viper is otherwise unmolested. The suspension, wheels, tires and braking systems are all as they were when the blood-engorged beast left New Mack Assembly in Detroit.

▶ Terror At The Strip

It only takes one jab at the throttle to know one modification this car really needs: back tires about six feet wide. With the 3.73 rear end and extra gobs of low-end torque, Hennessey's retro-rocket will annihilate the 335/35ZR17 rear treads even if you launch in third gear. First gear still works best to achieve the quickest acceleration times, but you'll walk a microscopic line between enough and too much wheelspin nearly the entire length of the strip.

It happens like this: You avoid the bleach box and do one long burnout followed by a couple of brief dry hops to test the available traction. Finding none, you roll up to the staging beams and try to concentrate on smoothness. Hah! It ain't in the cards, bucko. With the engine barely alive at idle, you release the long throw of the clutch in harmony with a slight application of throttle. Even at 700 rpm, there's enough torque here to pull a freight train over the Rockies. In an instant, the rear tires break loose and send the back end slewing wildly to the right. High-pitched tire squeal melds with a satanic whoosh from underhood as the beast within explodes into life. Ohmigod!

Okay, countersteer...give 'er steady throttle...keep it straight. But it's only good for an instant; the tach needle sweeps into the yellow and you grab second gear. A nanosecond later you're heading sideways, almost into the other lane. You respond just in time, but there are still two gears to go. Sixty mph happens in 4.3 seconds, and it takes every ounce of concentration to keep this thing in its lane, as you're now above 80 and the tires are still lit up, the rear end slewing ever-so-slightly right and left as the Michelins fight for every scrap of traction. Breathing is no longer an involuntary action. Your focus is suddenly on survival. Don't end up in a fireball and the day will be just fine, thank you.

The gate into third resists most attempts at speed shifting, but you deftly make the cog change, and then on into fourth an instant later. You blaze through the traps in 12.6 seconds at 116 mph, fighting no longer for traction, but to keep the wind from ripping your helmet off.

Only Evelyn Wood could read the above account faster than the Venom Viper took to accomplish it.

Compared to a production Viper, Hennessey's behemoth is only about a half-second quicker and four mph faster in the quarter-mile. But, you can't score this car merely by using a fifth wheel; using the seat of the pants, it feels more like two seconds and 20 mph and, unless you're going bracket racing, the sensation is what matters most. The Venom kit makes the difference between instant acceleration that merely flattens your eyeballs and that which drills them out the back of your head. (Granted, now, a run with drag slicks would assuredly be interesting.)

▶ The Builder

John Hennessey, the Houston-based company's owner, is a newcomer gaining a foothold in the aftermarket world. Having earned notice by twice annihilating the megabuck entries in the Nevada Silver State Challenge and establishing a class

Winning formula: Factory suspension, capable of .96g on the skidpad, is retained.

record at Bonneville with his breathed-on Mitsubishi 3000GT VR-4, this aggressive entrepreneur sold his thriving asbestos-removal business to concentrate on street cleaning instead. Hennessey Motorsports now supplies hi-po parts for not only the 3000GT/Stealth crowd but for cash-heavy Viper owners as well.

➤ Desert Development

Hennessey's first Venom test mule was a customer car built under a rush schedule to compete in last spring's running of the (recently renamed) BluBlocker Nevada 100: a 90-mile, full-throttle dyno pull of an event that often leaves more competitors scattered along the shoulder than flashing across the finish line. Mega power, tall final-drive gearing, a big gas tank and stable high-speed handling are the top four items on the "must have" list for success on the high-desert highway. The well-massaged Viper averaged in excess of 150 mph and finished without incident.

Plain and simple, Hennessey Motorsports' Venom 500 package is not for everyone. I even suspect that many Viper owners will find it too brutal for their tastes. But if you crave power to the point of blind hysteria, this car will supply it in wild, ravenous, flesh-tearing mouthfuls.

I want one. ∎

SPECIFICATIONS

➤ General
Vehicle type: front-engine, rear-wheel-drive 2-door targa coupe
Structure: composite body panels over tubular-steel spaceframe
Market as tested: United States
Base MSRP: $50,000 (stock Viper) + $14,500 (Hennessey modifications) = $64,500
Airbag: none

➤ Engine
Type: longitudinally-mounted V-10, aluminum block and heads
Displacement (cc): 7990
Bore x stroke (mm): 101.6 x 98.6
Compression ratio: 10.0:1
Claimed horsepower (bhp): 500 @ 5600 rpm
Claimed torque (lbs. ft.): 550 @ 3800
Intake system: electronic fuel injection
Valvetrain: two pushrod-operated overhead valves per cylinder

➤ Transmission
Type: 6-speed manual
Ratios:
- 1st: 2.66
- 2nd: 1.78
- 3rd: 1.30
- 4th: 1.00
- 5th: 0.74
- 6th: 0.50

Final drive: 3.73

➤ Dimensions
Curb weight (lbs.): 3476
Wheelbase (in.): 96.2
Track, f/r (in.): 59.6/60.6
Length (in.): 175.1
Width (in.): 75.7
Height (in.): 44.0
Fuel capacity (US gal.): 22.0

➤ Suspension, brakes, steering
Suspension, front: double wishbones with coil springs and antiroll bar
Suspension, rear: double wishbones with coil springs and antiroll bar
Steering type: rack and pinion, power assisted
Wheels, f/r (in.): 17x10/17x13, aluminum alloy
Tires, front: 275/40ZR-17
Tires, rear: 335/35ZR-17
Brakes, f/r: 13.0-inch ventilated disc/13.0-inch ventilated disc
ABS: none

➤ Performance
0-60 (sec.): 4.3
Top speed (mph): considerable
1/4 mile: 12.60 sec. @ 116.0 mph
Braking, 60-0 (ft.): 136
Braking, 80-0 (ft.): 243
EPA fuel economy (city/hwy): not considerable

DODGE VIPER R/T10

PHOTO BY RON SESSIONS

If you're looking for sensible family transportation, turn the page. This isn't a car for the timid. Simply put, the Viper is the biggest-engine, quickest-accelerating, shortest-braking and grippiest-handling car ever produced by Chrysler Corporation. Nothing—not one machine—built by Chrysler during the heyday of the musclecar can touch the Viper in all-around performance. Not the 426 Hemi-powered Dodge Challenger or the high-winged Daytona. Forget about the 440-cu-in. Plymouth Barracuda, as well.

In fact, few automobiles short of a Shelby Cobra can best a Viper's time from 0-60 mph (4.8 sec) or down the 1/4-mile (13.1 sec @ 109.0 mph). Brutally fast and shamelessly archaic, Viper is the Sasquatch of today's automotive marketplace. It's big and hairy and muscular and flat scary to hang onto. A strange juxtaposition of high-fashion styling and pure, unadulterated force. A combination of shameless excess and back-to-basics logic at the same time. A car that, clearly, is politically incorrect for these "green" times. In other words, a car you'd sell your left arm for.

The 2-seat roadster wears a fiberglass-composite body with forward tilting hood. Sticky 17-in. tires and massive 13-in.-diameter (without ABS) 4-wheel discs reside underneath. Squinty, designer headlamps and the Dodge-signature "gunsight" grille make the appropriate muscle statement, while functional sidepipes jutting out beneath the doors are far more muted in tone than you'd imagine (thank the government's tough noise standards for that one).

Unlike Chevy's Corvette, Chrysler's hot-rod roadster offers a real trunk–nearly 12 cu ft.–and a legroom-for-7-footers interior, though someone forgot to include minor items such as side windows and exterior door handles. (There is a drop-in top and side curtains.)

Powering the 4-wheel amusement park is an all-aluminum V-10. At 8.0 liters (488 cu in.) of displacement, torque is its thing: 450 lb-ft @ 3600 rpm. Horsepower is a stout 400 @ 4600 rpm, and redline is a lofty 6000 rpm. Power delivery is smoother than you'd expect from such a heftyweight of an engine, and the standard Borg-Warner T56 6-speed manual delivers precise gear changes. Though, with its 0.50:1 ratio top gear, and rear-end cogs of 3.08:1, 100 mph in top gear equates to a mere 2000 rpm. Theoretical top speed is, thus, 300 mph. Actual terminal velocity is closer to 165 mph.

Production of the 1992 Viper was limited to just over 200 units; for 1993 it'll jump to over 1000, depending on the number of orders. Black joins red on the color palette, and there'll be other hues later on. At its base price of $50,000, and considering its perform-or-die attitude, Viper isn't a car for everyman/woman. If, however, you're looking for a V-10 Sasquatch of your own, hop in.

SPECIFICATIONS

Base price, base model	$50,000	
Country of origin/assembly	U.S.A.	
Body/seats	conv/2	
Layout	F/R	
Wheelbase	96.2 in.	
Track, f/r	59.6/60.6 in.	
Length	175.1 in.	
Width	75.7 in.	
Height	43.9 in.	
Luggage capacity	11.8 cu ft	
Curb weight	3485 lb	
Fuel capacity	22.0 gal.	
Fuel economy (EPA), city/highway	13/22 mpg	
Base engine	400-bhp, ohv, V-10	
Bore x stroke	101.6 x 98.6 mm	
Displacement	7990 cc	
Compression ratio	9.1:1	
Horsepower, SAE net	400 bhp @ 4600 rpm	
Torque	450 lb-ft @ 3600 rpm	
Optional engine(s)	none	
Transmission	6M	
Suspension, f/r	ind/ind	
Brakes, f/r	disc/disc	
Tires	P275/40ZR-17f, P335/35ZR-17r	
Steering type	rack & pinion	
Turning circle	40.7 ft	
Warranty, years/miles:		
Bumper-to-bumper	1/12,000[1]	
Powertrain	7/70,000[1]	
Rust-through	7/100,000	
Passive restraint, driver's side	door belt	
Front passenger's side	door belt	

[1] combined 3/36,000 bumper-to-bumper and powertrain warranty optional at no extra cost

SUDDENLY, IT'S 1963

Taking Dodge's Viper GTS to its true roots

BY JOHN LAMM
PHOTOS BY THE AUTHOR

Right at home in the Road America paddock during the Chicago Historic Automobile Races, the Viper GTS, like its roadster sibling, harkens back to the great racing coupes of the Sixties. Unlike Augie Pabst's #7 Scarab, however, the GTS's greatest potential lies in the future, not the past.

How times do change. I'm looking down at a tradition. A bratwurst. Road America's finest, cushioned in a bun and smothered in onions, mustard and catsup. When I first began to visit Elkhart Lake's famous road circuit as a teenager 33 years ago, I ate these with impunity. Now all I can think about is how much cholesterol there must be in each brat. What would my doctor say?

Yup, times change, but traditions must be honored, so over the lips, over the gums....

Back then, Roger Penske and Jim Hall were young hot-shoe drivers, and Indy cars—with front-mounted Offy engines and only two forward speeds—would have had a dickens of a time getting around this 4-mile race course. Dan Gurney was still racing in Europe, and the name Toyota was an oddity in America. All that is certainly different today.

But some things haven't changed at all. Despite more than $4 million spent upgrading the race track for CART competition, Road America maintains its basic race-through-the-woods character. Top-ranked names around Road America back then were Augie Pabst and his Meister Brauser Scarab. The starting fields were filled with various Ferrari 250s, Triumphs, Porsches, and, on this horsepower course of long straights and 90-degree turns, Corvettes and Cobras.

If you were to visit the Chicago Historic Automobile Races each mid-July, you'd find that patch of history back in place. You can again see pre-Sting Ray Corvettes slide around turn 5, then launch up the hill and under the bridge named for them. Cobras run nose-to-tail through the esses up from Canada Corner. And Augie still comes roaring out of the woods and down to turn 5, his Scarab—the finest-looking American spe-

Many flashed a thumbs-up and others would lean over as I idled by and simply shout, "BUILD IT!"

cial ever made—still dropping its nose under braking.

When you enter Road America from the front gate, the road to the paddock crosses another tradition I hope will never change, the Bill Mitchell bridge. The late Bill Mitchell was the flamboyant—sometimes outrageous—head of styling at General Motors. He was the sort of executive who makes boards of directors cringe over what he might say or do next. When asked in the early Seventies why the exterior design of a small car is such a problem, Mitchell reportedly replied, "Because it's more difficult to tailor a suit for a dwarf." Bill Porter, who now heads Buick's exterior design studio II, recalls Mitchell once reacting to a bland front-end treatment by saying, "Porter, that car looks like if you opened the hood pigeons would fly out."

Mitchell may have been a character, but that's also a quality instilled in the cars produced during his long reign at GM, a laudible quality now too easily missed by quite a few automakers. Ask many of today's important young designers—American or European—to name favorite cars from their youth, and they often mention Mitchell cars.

Bill Mitchell was also a big fan of Elkhart Lake's Road America, and used races there as a place to conduct show car debuts. Upon arriving at the track, we'd look to see what new show Corvette or Corvair was on display in the paddock. The original Sting Ray? Mako Shark? Corvair Monza GT or SS? XP-700? Sometimes there would be a tent at the Pine Point Lodge for the show cars, and we'd haunt it for hours. We wondered what it must be like to idle through the paddock in one of those show machines and then do a lap of Road America. The stuff of dreams?

Not anymore. Not since I called Chrysler and asked if they'd be interested in having the Dodge Viper GTS coupe at the historic races. Happily they agreed, and we had a chance to spend a weekend with the most popular show car this side of, well, the Plymouth Prowler.

What's it like? Great, watching the spectators turn on to the GTS. Vipers—open or closed—are very much "guy" cars; you don't see many women ogling their shapes. But little boys jump with delight when they see the GTS. Young men give it that "some day…" stare. Older guys, those who look as though they could afford one, cut right to the chase: "Are they going to build it?" "Any idea of the price?" and "What's the difference between this and the production Viper?"

As to the last question, surprisingly little. Converting the Viper R/T into the GTS wouldn't be all that difficult. Chassis and drivetrain are stock, and with them come the V-10, its 400 bhp and 465 lb-ft of torque, and the Borg-Warner 6-speed manual gearbox. Suspension has upper and lower A-arms at both ends, and a reputation for providing a stable, flat-handling platform. Remember, we saw a near-record 0.96g on the skidpad with the fat-tired Viper R/T, which then got through the slalom in a very respectable 62.7 mph. Little reason that should change with the coupe.

First visual change to the GTS starts at the nose, where that huge RTM plastic hood adds a NACA duct to force air directly into the induction system. Louvers on the top of each fender vent air, adding downforce in combination with a new lip spoiler, though in the form we see it on the GTS the lip is probably too low to be practical.

Although the GTS's door skins are the standard items, the rest of the bodywork is new. The roof has Abarth-like bubbles to add headroom, while the back end tapers along bulging fenders and a glass hatchback to a tail spoiler shaped not unlike the Ferrari GTO's. The aluminum wheels are a new, aggressive open design that emphasizes the car's 4-wheel non-ABS disc brakes, though I'd love to see them in a satin finish rather than the chrome. Then there's that paint, the rich blue metallic with the pair of wide white stripes that reinforces the Cobra Daytona coupe connection.

With the new bodywork, the GTS is 2.7 in. longer and 4.7 in. taller than the stock roadster. What the roof also adds, of course, is weight. The glass hatch and the top—if the latter were done in plastic—would add some 250 lb, though with all that V-10 power, it's doubtful most drivers would bemoan (or even notice) the added weight, given the addition of all-weather protection. We got the R/T to 60 mph in 4.8 seconds, and could easily live with 5.2 in the coupe to get the hardtop. Our top speed with the roadster Viper was 160 mph, and Chrysler president Bob Lutz has suggested that the coupe, with potentially better aerodynamics, might be even faster. Better yet, some of those added pounds might be trimmed from the car's overall poundage in the ongoing program to remove weight from the basic Viper design.

There are other benefits with the hardtop—roll-up glass windows and, in production, a proper at-the-back-of-the-door latch—that Dodge would like to add to the roadster Viper, making it easier to justify the GT. What also appeals to

■ **GTO and GTS: Though three decades separate the two, the Viper and Ferrari seem lifted from the same age. Tom Gale's classic curves sweep seductively over the Viper's modern mechanicals.**

■ Abarth-like "double bubble" roof complements the Viper's basic shape. Although differences such as the louvered fenders, ducted hood and capped sidepipes abound, much of the GTS is only slightly modified from the production roadster. As a concession to civility, the coupe's interior boasts conventional door handles and roll-up windows.

Chrysler about the GT is the minimal investment needed to add the coupe to the line—though with the truckloads of dollars the company is currently having to pump into the new-car programs that pay the big bills, don't expect to see a production GTS for a few years.

Driving around the paddock, trundling along the lanes of parked race cars, gauging reactions from spectators is a nice bit of sport. Many flashed a thumbs-up and others would lean over as I idled by and simply shout, "BUILD IT!" Judging by the number of photos taken of the car, I wondered if there wasn't also someone shouting, "CAMERAS UP!" One young man followed us from one paddock to the next on a moped, a video camera pressed to his eye. Whenever we stopped, the GTS was swamped by race fans and the questions flew. Usual first query: "Is this the only one?" followed by, "They will make more, won't they?"

At the end of the day I took a lap with the GTS. Open the door, and the interior looks like it might be a tight fit getting in, but the only problem is worming your way into the tangle of the 5-point competition belts, which would not be a production item. Set into a flat-black dash are the stock Viper R/T's neatly laid-out gauges, here with black faces instead of production white. The seats are new and feel about right, with a firm grip around the love handles. Visibility is good front, sides and rear, but the view ahead is what we're here for, sighting down the long

> Twist the key, the V-10 quickly clears its throat....

tention was the exhaust note of the V-10. Some auto journalists just can't get used to the uneven-firing engine, but I'm a fan of that odd pulse. The sound gets even stranger in the R/T when you drive close to an Armco rail and the side pipes reflect the 5-cylinder beat from one side of the engine. The GTS is somewhat different because it has the European-style capped-off side pipes and a conventional exhaust routing, though inside you still hear the basso profundo hum of the duals.

In deference to track corner workers, who were packing up, and Chrysler's concerns about the GTS's zillion dollar paint job, we kept things calm on our lap. All the more time to enjoy the tour, through corner 1, down to the straight that leads through the woods to turn 5. Up under the Corvette bridge and turn left to the area of the carousel, to the long straight before Canada Corner, up through the esses, under the Bill Mitchell bridge and back to the start/finish straight. Over too soon, but not before offering a sense of what it would be like to go whistling around Road America in a GTS...part of that 30-year dream.

It could have been 1993 or 1963. Other than engine electronics, development time and tire sizes, there's little fundamental mechanical difference between the Viper

■ Stock Viper mechanicals need no excuse: 400 bhp and 475 lb-ft of torque, driven through a smooth-shifting 6-speed gearbox.

hood with its twin white stripes. Twist the key, the V-10 quickly clears its throat and settles into that soothing rumble. Engage 1st gear, and with all that torque you barely touch the gas as you let out on the relatively light clutch.

Easy as pie. We're off to the track.

On the way, I stopped along the pit lane to pick up a passenger: our hero, Augie Pabst. First thing that caught Augie's at-

GTS and the best GTs of 30 years ago. The engine is still up front and runs on gasoline. It's a manual transmission. No ABS brakes, traction control or active suspension. Most important of all, perhaps, all the sensations are right...what you hear, smell and feel are simple and basic and they stir something good inside you.

Makes you wonder about progress.

I recently heard an excellent talk by the aforementioned Bill Porter describing GM show cars, beginning with the famous 1938 Buick Y-Job. Porter touched on the advancements of the XP-300, the LeSabre, the Wildcats, the Centurion, all show machines meant to pilot us straight into the future. All in the name of progress.

That laser-pace progression can be wonderful. Medical breakthroughs. Advanced computers. Fuzzy logic. Information at a dizzying rate...but maybe a bit too fast. And while that rush of information contains the good stuff, it also transports the bad, splashed in your face on video tape that was shot with a little hand-held camcorder. A wonder of technological progress recording our lack of social progress.

Production automobiles today burn less fuel, create less smog and have more performance than before, but many are just not soul-stirring. Too often they are formed in wind tunnels and board rooms, so the cars suffer from a boring sameness. Bill Mitchell would never approve.

So we can be forgiven if, in some aspects of our lives, we climb down off the leading edge of technology and fall head over heels for a sensuous automobile like the Viper GTS, one that proves that progress doesn't require a complete break with the past, and epitomizes why so many of the exotic cars in this issue have retro-theme styling.

Let's hear it for traditional thinking. And let's have another bratwurst. ■

■ Even in non-production form, the GTS weighs a mere 250 lb more than the production roadster. Improved aerodynamics offset the added weight with an increase over the stock car's 160-mph top speed.

DODGE VIPER GTS

SPECIFICATIONS

Curb Weight	3724 lb
Wheelbase	96.2 in.
Track, f/r	59.6 in./60.6 in.
Length	177.8 in.
Width	75.7 in.
Height	48.7 in.
Fuel capacity	20 gal.

ENGINE & DRIVETRAIN

Engine	ohv V-10
Bore x stroke	101.6 mm x 98.5 mm
Displacement	7990 cc
Compression ratio	9.1:1
Horsepower, SAE net	400 bhp @ 4600 rpm
Torque	465 lb-ft @ 3600 rpm
Fuel injection	electronic port
Transmission	6-sp manual
Final-drive ratio	3.07:1

CHASSIS & BODY

Layout	front engine/rear drive
Brake system, f/r	13.0-in. ventilated disc/ 13.0-in. ventilated disc, vacuum assist
Wheels	light alloy, 17 x 10.5 f, 17 x 13.0 r
Tires	Michelin XGT 2, P275/40ZR-17 f, P335/35ZR-17 r
Steering type	rack & pinion, power assisted
Suspension, f/r	upper and lower A-arms, coil springs, tube shocks, anti-roll bar/upper and lower A-arms, toe links, coil springs, tube shocks, anti-roll bar

PERFORMANCE[1]

0-60 mph	5.2 sec
Standing 1/4 mile	13.2 @ 110 mph
Top speed	165 mph

[1]Manufacturer's claims.

Hennessey Motorsports Venom 500 Viper

Mad As a Snake

Only America could produce a car as brutal and politically incorrect as the Dodge Viper, which with 400bhp, is hardly undernourished. And only in America could this be not enough to be going on with. Craig Peterson drives the Hennessey Viper

Critics of the Dodge Viper complain that it reeks of excess: too many cubic inches, too much exhaust racket and wind noise, too much power. To their horror, tuner John Hennessey has slyly produced what he calls the Venom 500, a Viper that goes even further — it's pumped up from 400bhp to 500bhp with torque elevated from 450lb ft to a lofty 550lb ft. And by special request, he will build a Venom which generates closer to 600bhp. That's real automotive excess.

Consider this: it managed sixty in 3.8 seconds (normal Viper does 4.4) and whistled through the quarter mile in 12.2 seconds at 120mph (13.1secs/108mph), despite the fact that it is so traction-limited its massive 335/40 ZR17 rear Michelins did not stop spinning until the middle of fourth gear and 105mph.

The man responsible, John Hennessey, is becoming known as a thoughtful, methodical tuner, capable of producing non-temperamental but vastly more powerful versions of some already fast machinery. In the Venom 500 he follows conventional techniques to coax more from the 8-litre aluminium V10, a derivative of Dodge's cast iron truck engine. The intake manifold is treated to a process in which fine abrasives are blasted through it to increase volume and smooth rough edges. Larger throttle bodies are fitted, breathing through low restriction air filter elements. The two-valve-per-cylinder alloy heads are milled for greater compression, intake and exhaust ports are gas-flowed and polished and low-restriction roller rocker arms with a 1.7:1 ratio, up from the stock 1.6, provide greater lift. Guide plates and hardened pushrods keep geometry correct at the

● Viper looks standard but has tweaked guide plates, hardened pushrods and a dual engine management system

engine's elevated operating speeds, doubly necessary on our test car as it was fitted with an experimental camshaft sporting much higher lift and longer duration.

The radical camshaft proved a headache for engine wizard Robin St. John who was forced to rely on an adjustable auxiliary fuel-mixture computer piggy-backed to the stock ECM (the engine management system can't be reprogrammed) to achieve civilised levels of driveability.

Stainless steel tubular headers replace factory cast-iron exhaust manifolds and lead to low-restriction aftermarket catalytic converters, then into enormous side pipes which exit just below the doors. The engine's swept volume produces a hurricane exhaust sufficient to sweep clean an average-sized driveway merely by backing out of the garage. As a final touch Hennessey replaces the stock 3.07 final drive with a 3.73 ratio, making the overdrive fifth and sixth gears far more useful.

According to Hennessey the Viper's Borg Warner six-speed transmission is comfortably robust enough to handle the new power levels. In addition, the suspension remains unchanged (double-wishbones at each corner with coil springs and tubular dampers), and the standard 13-inch diameter four-wheel vented discs remain as well. Standard 17-inch XGT-Z Michelins in sizes 275/40 front and 335/40 rear (the widest available) ride on factory alloy wheels 10.5 inches and 13 inches wide.

En route to our drag strip session it was clear that Hennessey's modifications were a success in producing more horsepower without destroying response. The bad-boy camshaft suffers from occasional low-speed hiccups and a tendency to lope at idle, but the stiffer rear gearing served to launch the 488 cubic inch engine quickly into its power band. In truth, it delivers such prodigious low-speed torque the best technique for departing from rest is to leave your foot off the accelerator entirely and simply engage the clutch at idle. Adding even a whiff of power results in smoking burn-outs — Hennessey admits he's been unable to get a power reading on this car but in its only visit to a chassis dynamometer it pegged the needles while still fully 1000rpm below the power peak. At which point it began to shred its rear tyres.

The engine note is fine

81

Hennessey Motorsports Venom 500 Viper

● With 500bhp and enough torque to move the Himalayas, the Hennessey Viper does not leave the line too smoothly

at speed but in town it's noisy — those who haven't experienced this V10 will find it sounds distinctly agricultural. Fortunately a new $5000 carbon-Kevlar hardtop makes the cockpit quieter, and Hennessey is developing proper windows to replace the drafty current items.

Despite the occasional inadvertent burn-outs at stop lights the Venom 500 is enormously entertaining to drive and acceleration at any speed is awesome. On winding two-lane highways it's little more difficult to drive than a standard saloon — at least until you toe the throttle. Hennessey's stout camshaft abruptly comes to life at 4000rpm, bringing perhaps another 100bhp to the party and sending the big V10 rocketing towards its 6200rpm red line. This sudden blast of power can be distressing to the unwary, particularly in curves, as the rear tyres will lighten up at speeds well past the ton mark.

We'd advise against sideways motoring on roads of normal dimensions — the Viper is 76 inches wide.

The best part of the Venom 500 experience, though, is found on the open road where its long legs and comfortable ride allow effortless high speed cruising. With over 400lb ft available from just off idle through 5000rpm, a downshift for overtaking isn't really required. The lower final drive makes fifth and sixth gear acceleration more lively. While a standard Viper gets winded as it nears its 4600rpm power peak, the energised Venom 500 continues to generate useful thrust for fully 1400rpm beyond that. Under acceleration the Venom's B-17 exhaust note, frequently coupled with the racket from the spinning rear tyres, makes it difficult to aurally monitor engine speed. The 6200rpm rev limiter is vital.

Hennessey's hard-top serves to smooth the air flow, lowering interior sound levels and probably delivering an improved Cd figure. While a normal Viper achieves a maximum of 163mph in fifth gear, a Venom 500 *sans* killer camshaft and lacking the hard-top has been clocked at 170 mph, attained in sixth gear at 4800rpm. With the slicked-up aerodynamics and an extra 100bhp on hand, our test car could likely crack 180mph, a figure we were unable to verify due to adverse conditions. But full-chat top speed is not this car's forte: its neck-straining acceleration is the really big news.

The beauty of the Venom 500 lies in its price-to-performance ratio. Hennessey's modifications add $22,500 to the base Viper's $62,000 list price, creating a genuine supercar for a fraction of the cost of a Diablo or 512TR. Okay, perhaps it doesn't offer quite the panache of the more established brands and its truck-derived 20-valve pushrod V10 may be a bit industrial, but who cares? The Venom 500 delivers exactly what tuner John Hennessey intends: budget-priced rocket sled performance calculated to put a wicked gleam in your eye. ○

DATA FILE

Engine	ten cylinders in vee, longitudinal
Max Power	500bhp@6000rpm
Max Torque	550lb ft@5000rpm
0-60MPH	3.8secs
Max Speed	180mph (approx)
Standing 1/4mile	12.2
Price	$85,000 (approx)

DODGE
VIPER RT/10
Instant outlaw—just add throttle
BY RICHARD HOMAN
PHOTOS BY GUY SPANGENBERG

It's an attitude. An American rebel's attitude. And the Dodge Viper RT/10 roadster has it, that in-your-face (as in "wind-in-your-face") attitude. Imagine "The Star Spangled Banner" written by Guns N' Roses, and you'll get a clear vision of the Viper's unflinching disposition. It's *Lollapalooza '94* on wheels.

The path of the Viper's brief history is deeply trodden—word-worn by the buff books—but we shall pass along it once more, albeit quickly.

The Viper RT/10 began life as a Chrysler concept car at a time when the carmaker was in dire need of a concept. The 1989 Detroit auto show hosted the Viper's debut, and immediately the press

> **You can blather on about low-tech design, pushrods and two valves per cylinder; the Viper engine is the Torque of the Town.**

corps drums began a steady beat of "build it, build it, build it." The enthusiast public followed with its chorus of encouragement. Chrysler, realizing that it was a company kept afloat by minivans, and finding that this was the ideal image maker to see it through until the LH sedans and Neon subcompacts were ready, decided to do something about it. A "Team Viper" skunk works group of motorhead volunteers began working evenings and weekends to develop the dream, with Chrysler President Bob Lutz in the Mickey Rooney role ("Hey gang! Let's put on a show!...I mean a sports car!").

Three years later, in the spring of 1992, those kids rolled out one hell of an uncompromising show—I mean sports car. The idea

was to create a simple, Spartan, purpose-built super-roadster for the Nineties, as much a nod to Carroll Shelby and his 427 Cobra as anything else. Chassis, drivetrain, body—period. The root proof is in the power and the wind-swept grin of the Viper driver. Forget the roll-up windows (it's got side curtains); forget exterior door handles (reach in); forget trick top mechanisms (just leave the roof at home); forget the big trunk (drive this, carry groceries in the Tercel); and forget factory-installed air conditioning and a Nakamichi stereo (okay, it *does* get factory a/c as an option this year). Give it an austere interior with super-supportive bucket seats, a man's man's steering wheel, readable gauges (black numbers on a light-gray face by day, yellow-lit numbers on a black background by night) and a basic heating system, and you've pretty much peaked as a Viper interior designer.

The heart of a Viper, of course, is the legend in the engine bay: the 400-horsepower all-aluminum 8.0-liter V-10 engine, the cast-iron version of which can be found in the top 1994 Dodge Ram pickups. You can blather on all you want about low-tech design, pushrods and two valves per cylinder; the Viper engine is the

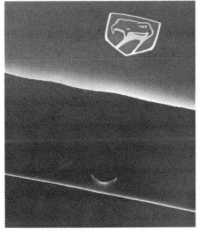

Torque of the Town.

Thanks go to both Chrysler and Lamborghini engineers for wrenching 450 lb-ft of torque from the 7990-cc engine, with a generous slathering of cranking power distributed from 1500 to 5500 rpm. By my gauges, a 1500-rpm cruise in top gear of the Borg-Warner 6-speed manual gearbox produces a cool 70 mph. But reality testing is done in 1st, 2nd and 3rd gears with all that cataclysm cut loose to the rear wheels through a 3.07:1 limited-slip diff and the tach needle hell-bent for the 6000-rpm redline.

The engine's 10-cylinder song is not really one of beauteous euphony, but a bit more like that of a V-12 with a hangover. During the photo shoot, I never had to alert the photographer that I was coming—my syncopation always preceded me, as it were. Not complaining, though. The Viper bellows with an enthusiastic, carnivorous growl, completely in line with the car's visceral character. And it'll kill, clean, skin and cook just about everything else out there.

We're not just talking straight-line stuff here, either. Through the nine turns of Willow Springs Raceway, the RT/10's cornering grip was phenomenal in a race-car kind of way: It sticks to the tarmac right up to its supercar-adhesion limit with very little early warning of slip. Nuzzling beyond that limit—or taking advantage of the Viper's willingness to tuck into a corner on lift-throttle—requires a tight hand on the reins. The Viper weighs less than a ZR-1 Corvette, yet it is connected to the road by a bigger patch of rubber than any other production car in the world: 275/40ZR-17s in front, 335/35ZR-17s at the rear (Michelin XGT2s). And the massive discs of the Viper's non-anti-lock brakes are just as serious about their job as the tires are about theirs.

A steel tube frame, clothed in a fiberglass-and-aluminum body, serves as the foundation for this

PHOTO LOCATION COURTESY COOKS CORNER, TRABUCO CANYON, CALIFORNIA

Gibraltar-solid roadster. This raceresque setup is garnished by a truck-solid (and, indeed, Dakota-derived) independent double A-arm suspension, with Koni gas coil-over shocks and fore-and-aft anti-roll bars. The suspension teams with the Viper's super-feel, quick/sharp/direct, power-assisted steering to provide the driver with a Technicolor presentation of the rhythms of the road.

Cobra of the Nineties? Shelve that nostalgia. The magic formula here is performance matched by beauty. Plenty of people who have never heard of Carroll Shelby and wouldn't know a Cobra from a Mongoose still get a tingling in their nether regions when a Viper passes by. Why? It could be that awesome snake's-head visage in the Viper's head-on view. Or the sensuous, liquid lines of the front fenders. Maybe it's the engine-venting gills or the brash, brilliant sidepipes. And perhaps the appeal is in the overall gut hit of the Viper's wide stance and its low, low profile. Car junkies talk about the Viper's lines in the same admiring tones they used to reserve

for Ferraris. Nostalgia? Not yet.

Instant celebrity. That's what the Viper offers. More than *any* other American car on the road. What about the Corvette? Certainly a Vette owner will never be found wanting for friends. Chevrolet's V-8 wonderwork endures as America's premier sports car, with a well-deserved share of automotive groupies. The problem is that my new Corvette looks just like yours and just like that other guy's over there. Where's the distinction? Where's the status? Where's the celebrity?

Okay, so what about the Vector? Well, the Vector W8 TwinTurbo is a stunning American supercar project, and a king-hell inspiration to performance lovers everywhere. But the Vector is the Elvis of sports cars—everybody, including the enlightened legions of the

automotive press wants to believe the sightings are real, but it's hard to put any faith in them. Especially now that after a tormented incubation of nearly 20 years, the poor-little-rich Vector is having a harder childhood than the Menendez brothers.

The Dodge Viper, on the other hand, is The Real Thing. An outlaw that went from Motown to your town in just 36 months. The face on everybody's wanted poster. And the price on its head—check with your dealer—is comparable to that of a Corvette ZR-1.

Next up in Viperland: The open-air RT/10 gets a hardtop brother. Equally cool and equally libertine as its roadster sibling, the Dodge Viper GTS Coupe has been given the go-ahead for production (Chrysler wants to clear its books of roadster orders before it starts selling the Coupes). So in 1996, Frank and Jesse will ride again.

DODGE
VIPER RT/10

PRICE
List price, all POE......................$50,000
Price as tested $54,880
Price as tested includes std equip. (AM/FM stereo/cassette, heater), gas guzzler tax ($2100), dest charge ($700), luxury tax ($2080).

ENGINE
Type	ohv V-10
Displacement	7990 cc
Bore x stroke	101.6 x 98.6 mm
Compression ratio	9.1:1
Horsepower, SAE net	400 bhp @ 4600 rpm
Torque	450 lb-ft @ 3600 rpm
Maximum engine speed	6000 rpm
Fuel injection	electronic port
Fuel requirement	premium unleaded

GENERAL DATA
Curb weight	3475 lb
Test weight	3635 lb
Weight distribution, f/r, %	49/51
Wheelbase	96.2 in.
Track, f/r	59.6/60.6 in.
Length	175.1 in.
Width	75.7 in.
Height	43.9 in.
Trunk space	11.8 cu ft

CHASSIS & BODY
Layout	front engine/rear drive
Body/frame	fiberglass+aluminum/tubular steel
Brakes, f/r	13.0-in. vented discs/13.0-in. vented discs, vacuum assist
Wheels	welded cast/spun-alloy, 17 x 10 f, 17 x 13 r
Tires	Michelin XGT2 P275/40ZR-17 f, P335/35ZR-17 r
Steering	rack & pinion, power assist
Turns, lock to lock	2.4
Suspension, f/r	upper & lower A-arms, coil springs, tube shocks, anti-roll bar/upper & lower A-arms, toe links, coil springs, tube shocks, anti-roll bar

DRIVETRAIN
Transmission .... 6-sp manual

Gear	Ratio	Overall Ratio	(Rpm)	Mph
1st	2.66:1	8.17:1	(6000)	56
2nd	1.78:1	5.46:1	(6000)	84
3rd	1.30:1	3.99:1	(6000)	115
4th	1.00:1	3.07:1	(6000)	150
5th	0.74:1	2.27:1	(4750)	160
6th	0.50:1	1.54:1	est (3210)	160

Final-drive ratio 3.07:1
Engine rpm @ 60 mph, top gear ...... 1200 rpm

ACCELERATION
Time to speed	seconds
0-30 mph	2.0
0-40 mph	2.7
0-50 mph	3.6
0-60 mph	4.8
0-70 mph	5.8
0-80 mph	7.6
0-90 mph	9.2
0-100 mph	11.1
Time to distance	
0-100 ft	na
0-500 ft	na
0-1320 ft (1/4 mile)	13.1 sec @ 109.0 mph

BRAKING
Minimum stopping distance
From 60 mph	156 ft
From 80 mph	201 ft
Control	very good
Overall brake rating	good

HANDLING
Lateral accel (200-ft skidpad)	0.96g
Speed thru 700-ft slalom	62.7 mph

FUEL ECONOMY
Normal driving	12 mpg
Fuel economy (EPA city/highway)	13/22 mpg
Fuel capacity	22.0 gal.

est estimated, na means information not available

COUPE DE PACE

Surely no American car in recent times has created the sort of sensation as the Dodge Viper when it was announced. Now, with the new coupe version about to go into production, the superlatives will start all over again. Phil Carter drove the prototype, Peter Robain photographed it

Only the Americans could do it. Only they could just let their imaginations run wild to produce the Viper. Combining brute power from its 8 litre V10 engine with a composite-plastic body whose looks make your eyes, let alone your mouth water. It was a knock-out when the original Viper RT/10 was wheeled out of the styling studio by proud Chrysler personnel a few years back.

Of course, in the politically correct days of the early Nineties, no-one even contemplated the car would ever see production, but when, late in '92 Chrysler boss Bob Lutz announced that (a) it was going to be built and (b) it was coming to Britain via the newly set up Chrysler-Jeep Imports, sports car enthusiasts from both sides of the Atlantic began to quiver with excitement.

The response was electric, moreso even than Lutz himself had expected. He reasoned that such a reaction should never go unheeded, and thus it was only a matter of months before Chrysler trumped everything at the 1993 Los Angeles Auto Show with the Viper GTS Coupe.

Inspired by the '65 Shelby Daytona sports-racer, Chrysler had done it again, and this time it was with the co-operation of that legend of American sports car design, Carroll Shelby. It was he who had sanctioned the original design of the Daytona for entry in that year's Le Mans 24 hour race. Styled by Peter Brock, one of Shelby's first employees, it won the World Manufacturers' Championship at the race and thus passed into the history books.

The Viper GTS marked the beginning of a new dawn for the US motor industry, for too many years bogged down with staid designs and a reputation for lacklustre styling, low levels of

> *"...there just isn't one single angle from which it looks wrong."*

innovation and poor quality.

If you could dream the looks of the Coupe, they wouldn't come any more 'right' than this. From nose to screen, it's all RT/10 but there the similarities end. Taking his styling cues from a host of Italian design houses, Chrysler's director of advanced and international design, Neil Walling, created a roof with a characteristic 'double-bubble' top - that is with visible swellings above driver and passenger. It extended back to a deep bootlid spoiler that surrounded the tail, highlighting the stock lamps and rear bumper. The windscreen was raised

Top above: *At speed on the banked track Viper GTS looks right at home. Rear glass canopy and spoiler give car an attractive back end plus some decent luggage capacity*
Right: *Chrysler promise V10 8 litre engine will be even more powerful when the coupe goes into production - that's over 400 bhp!*
Above: *Interior is very similar to Viper roadster, but production coupe will be better equipped and won't have competition safety harness*
Left: *'Double-bubble' roof contour can be plainly seen from this angle, Viper GTS Coupe is a stunner from any viewpoint*

COUPE DE PACE

to meet the new roof's leading edge, and in all the car sits some five inches higher than the roadster.

The transformation was done with minimal change to the original design - key to the successful graduation to production. The doors, dash and interior were untouched, but the coupe adopted a sense of practicality missing from the convertible and will come with some extra comforts.

The whole car was topped off with a deep metallic blue paint job, punctuated by two broad white stripes running down the middle - just like the original Daytona. It carried the essence of that car reproduced faithfully and authentically for the Nineties.

Under the stunning skin, of course, the mechanicals are all Viper RT/10, but then, with over 400 bhp and 465 lb fit of torque at just 3600 rpm, who needs more? Well, Chrysler have promised the production GTS Coupe will have more! More than enough to improve on the roadster's 0-60 mph accceleration of 4.5 seconds and top speed of 166 mph.

The GTS does away with the characteristic side pipes for its exhaust system. They're there of course, just for looks, but both are blanked off in favour of a pair of drainpipes connecting without silencers or catalysts straight to the engine.

The car rides on ultra-wide, fabricated chrome-plated wheels, handmade for this prototype and shod with enormous Michelin low-profile tyres. As it sits quietly in the morning sunshine at Chrysler's test track in Detroit there isn't one single angle from which it looks wrong.

I'm here to drive this most beautiful of cars, in the presence of designer Neil Walling. He warns me that it is just a prototype, that most of the special parts, including those wheels, are handmade and that it is essentially just for show. I'm limited to a top speed of 60 mph as the wheels are not properly balanced and can't be used for extensive high speed circuit work. But above all, this is the only example in existence. If I stuffed it, there would be no Viper GTS left in the world!

With that indelibly stamped on my mind, I opened the door and slide in. It's all just like the original Viper inside: there's a five-point harness for both driver and passenger, but head and legroom are good. The bubble roof would easily accept a helmet should

"It's not a peaky, temperamental delivery, just a solid wall of urge..."

the GTS ever be used in competition, and a look over my right shoulder confirms that a long Continental journey would be entirely possible such is the luggage room available under the glass hatch.

Turn the key and the massive motor rumbles into life. With the straight-through exhaust, you can virtually hear each firing stroke from the paint-pot-sized pistons as they thump up and down at idle. It's loud with a capital 'L', but a strangely unfamiliar sound. The only V10 engine fitted to a current road car, it revs with more of a blare than a howl or a roar. With a muted exhaust system, as fitted to the roadster, it is an impressive but relatively unexciting sound.

With so much torque available from tickover, you can move off in any of the gearbox's six speeds save top itself. That's geared for a monumental 53.3 mph per 1000 rpm - which means you could break the US speed limit at a little above tickover!

Depressing the clutch and selecting first gear, it's surprising how light the transmission action is. You don't need the muscles of Arnold Schwarzenegger to do either, which is unusual considering the duties each has to perform to tame all that power and torque.

Edge out on to the smooth surface of the track and before you know it the engine is crying out for more gears. You oblige, while at the same time listening to the blast of the exhaust as the revs rise and fall. In any gear, the acceleration is awesome. Floor it in third at 1000 rpm and you are hurled back in your seat as all 465 lb ft of torque goes to work. It's not a peaky, temperamental delivery, just a solid wall of urge that leaves you wondering why they ever needed to fit a gearbox in the first place.

The engine will run smoothly all the way to 6000 rpm, at which point it's best not to think about the kind of inertia that's generated by the movement of those massive pistons. In any case, there's little point in revving so hard as maximum power comes in at just 4600 rpm and there is easily enough torque in reserve to blast you past anything.

The steering is sharp and responsive, heavily power-assisted with so much weight over the front wheels, and the car changes direction with precision and very little roll.

With fully independent suspension

FACTFILE

1994 DODGE VIPER GTS
2-Door Sports Coupe

Engine:
Overhead valve V10, aluminium block and heads
Capacity: 488 cu.in. (8.0 litres)
Bore and stroke: 4.0 x 3.87 inches
Compression ratio: 9.1:1
Max horsepower: 400+ at 4600 rpm
Max torque: 465 foot pounds at 3600 rpm
Induction: Multi-point Fuel Injection

Transmission:
Borg Warner 6-speed manual

Chassis/Body:
Wheelbase: 96.2 inches
Overall length: 175.1 inches
Overall width: 75.7 inches
Height: 49.0 inches
Suspension: Independent front and rear with unequal length control arms, coil springs and Koni dampers all round
Wheels: Aluminium alloy, 10 x 17 inches (front), 13 x 17 inches (rear)
Tyres: Michelin 275/40ZR17 (front), 335/35ZR17 (rear)

Performance:
Top speed: 166 mph+
0-60 mph: 4.5 seconds
Standing quarter mile: 12.79 seconds at 110 mph

General:
Approx 1996 UK price: £65,000

all round - double wishbones, coil springs, anti-roll bars and adjustable Koni dampers at both front and rear - there's no problem getting the power down, though it's possible to spin the massive 13 inch wide rear tyres into smoke-filled oblivion with enthusiastic use of the throttle - even in third gear. To do so would necessitate new ones every 1000 miles or so, and at several hundred pounds a throw, such foolishness is best avoided.

I managed to see about 80 mph on the straight before my conscience gripped me and I backed off to save the tyres. With windows rolled up and the car in sixth, it's respectably quiet and relaxed, though at these sorts of speeds you've only got some 1500 rpm on the tacho. Even so, acceleration is vivid at the merest touch of the throttle.

All too soon it was time to pull in. Stepping from the driver's seat and glancing back confirmed that the GTS is certainly one of the most handsome cars in the world. Word from Chrysler has it that, following the usual period of 'gauging public reaction', production plans are now in hand for the super coupe, with the UK launch provisionally set for January '96.

In the words of Peter Brock, designer of the original Shelby: "The car is so well finished, they're really looking at it from a production standpoint." That being the case, you can mark my words it'll outsell the roadster.

COVER **CAR AND DRIVER** STORY

THE SUPERCAR OLYMPICS

Introducing five predatory athletes from five countries, all with carnivorous appetites. They'll eat your lunch, your wallet, possibly you, too.

BY JOHN PHILLIPS

PHOTOGRAPHY BY DAVID DEWHURST

In 1897, Captain S.A. Swiggett wrote a book called *The Bright Side of Prison Life*. It occurred to me to take a copy to southern Ohio, where we were testing five supercars, any one of which could get me arrested while cruising in *second* gear on eastern interstates. Our assault on Ohio's scenic Hocking Hills would be swift and international in flavor. In total, we had 1745 horsepower on tap, from $472,000 worth of exotica. And our five supercar contestants represented five countries: America (Dodge Viper RT/10), Germany (Porsche 911 Turbo) Great Britain (Lotus Esprit S4S), Italy (Ferrari F355), and Japan (Acura NSX-T). Think of it as the Olympics of supercars.

The newest weaponry on the supercar scene—the Porsche and Ferrari—triggered this comparison test. In making our other selections, there seemed no good reason to include anything with a price higher than the Ferrari's $128,800, and all five voting editors agreed it wouldn't have changed the outcome anyway. Before the Anglophiles complain, remember that the McLaren F1 is not legal here. Subscribers enamored of Italian machinery should note that the Ferrari F50 isn't ready yet, and no Bugatti EB110 has yet been sold in America. Red-white-and-blue patriots should similarly recall that the Corvette ZR-1, which admittedly would have been a better-rounded ambassador than the Dodge Viper, went the way of the passenger pigeon one month before this story would appear.

Our vehicles thus assembled, it was curious to discover that, quite without trying, we wound up with no similar engine architectures. The engines include a single-turbo in-line four, a twin-turbo flat-six, a DOHC V-6, a 40-valve V-8, and a pushrod V-10. The Lotus, the Ferrari, and the NSX are mid-engined. The Porsche is rear-engined. The Viper is front-engined. From a styling standpoint—at least according to Ohio and Michigan citizens who rushed us at every fuel stop—not one of these vehicles looks very much like any other.

So what did we hope to discover in one week of driving? We needed to know which was the fastest, and we found out after just one day at Ohio's sprawling Transportation Research Center. The intangibles were trickier. Which car is easiest to drive at nine-tenths on public roads? Which impresses onlookers most? Which is the most fun to drive, never mind its performance envelope? Which is the most potent and comfortable long-distance tourer? Which is the most passionate? Which feels the least likely to spend its life atop a service hoist?

THE SUPERCAR OLYMPICS

It took a week of nonstop driving and late-night arguing to find out, during which interval we pushed the vehicles hard enough that both the NSX and the Viper had to be retrieved from ditches. Said *C/D* godfather Brock Yates, as he brushed pieces of hemlock bough and sandstone grit off his vest: "At about 90 percent of their capabilities, all five of these cars are hugely competent and benign, lulling their drivers into Fangio-like confidence. But put one toe over the edge and there's an excellent chance you'll get to help refurnish your insurance agent's new home in Grosse Pointe."

Or, to put it another way, begin memorizing passages from *The Bright Side of Prison Life*.

Fifth Place
Lotus Esprit S4S

Twenty years ago, our first test of a Lotus Esprit offered this keen insight: "The factory is frank about the Esprit's unsuitability for grand touring... the twin tanks should be filled with gas destined to be burned in bursts of back-road berserking."

Not much has changed in two decades, although thanks to a larger Garrett turbo and larger inlet valves, the Lotus's maniacally peaky 2.2-liter four-banger now delivers an even more berserk steady-state 285 hp and briefly as much as 300 hp, if the weather on Route 595 near Logan, Ohio, is sufficiently cool and dry. When the turbo kicks in at around 2700 rpm, it's like being smacked in the back of the head with a warped nine-iron. A kind of blurry trauma ensues. Full boost in the rain will light up the rear tires in first, second, and third gears. At which point, the Esprit's tail yaws right on crowned roads, the driver countersteers like Damon Hill, then the whole mess straightens out after a vicious snap that leaves onlookers wondering if you've lost your mind or are just insanely rich. Or both.

The 60-mph barrier topples in 4.4 seconds, making the Esprit quicker in a straight line than a 405-hp Corvette ZR-1, which possibly did not amuse Detroit engineers back when GM owned Lotus.

There is much about the Esprit that is race-car-like. The pedals are skewed inboard and are so close together that Simpson's best Nomex booties are recommended. The steering is knife-like and fast,

LOTUS ESPRIT S4S

Highs: Efficient and potent engine, neutral handling, still a dazzling silhouette.

Lows: Hunt-and-peck shifter, shoebox cockpit, dreadful visibility.

The Verdict: Aging but lithe Brit in search of dedicated Anglophile enthusiasts.

although it is a great match for the car's flat, neutral cornering stance. Once you push through the surging and sucking power assist for the Brembo brakes, you have exactly the pedal feel you'd want in Turn One at Long Beach.

Far less race-ready is the Renault-based gear linkage, a high-effort yet mushy affair. "It's like making a long-distance call to Paris to make a gearchange," says Kevin Smith. It is also fragile, not a good trait in turbo cars, which encourage quick shifting to keep the boost on the boil. This may explain why second gear was no longer with us at the end of this test. Similarly unrefined is the Esprit's powerplant, which bangs and bucks as if it were a 2.2-liter K-car engine forced to produce the highest specific output of any in-line four in America. Not a far-fetched analogy.

Still, the Esprit's cuneiform figure—its waist-high profile, even its gaudy wing that overreaches the rear bumper—makes onlookers gawk and chase, although they rarely know what they're looking at. They mouth the word "Lotus," then say, "Oh, the *Pretty Woman* car." But they always assume that it costs more than its $80,340 base.

Cranky, quirky, and as breakable as Waterford crystal, the Lotus finished last but by only two points. It is eccentric (hell, when did you last hear of a supercar getting a 27-mpg EPA highway rating?), a lean point-and-squirt machine for nasty, unpredictable roads. Such as the wicked little lanes around Norwich. Think of it as half Formula Ford made street-legal, half Barbara Woodhouse on PCP.

Fourth Place
Dodge Viper RT/10

The Dodge Viper is the antithesis of the Lotus. Where the Lotus is a kind of .22-caliber Olympic target pistol, the Viper is simply an 16-inch cannon yanked off the deck of the *USS Missouri*. The Lotus is the lightest car in the group, the Viper is the heaviest. The Lotus has the smallest engine in the group, the Viper's 488-cube thunderbox is the most mammoth passenger-car powerplant in production. The Lotus offers the fastest lane-change capability, the Viper possesses the slowest.

Yet in this comparo, the Viper occupies fourth place rather than fifth. Here are three reasons: (1) big torque exists at *any* engine revolution, (2) its shape evokes involuntary seizures among all onlookers, and (3) it has the lowest sticker price in *all* of supercardom.

DODGE VIPER RT/10

Highs: Thor's own torque, convertible top; a gawker magnet.

Lows: Mixmaster ride, ragged assembly, knife-in-the-back handling.

The Verdict: Blockbuster mystique that surpasses its price but also its real usefulness.

Of course, there are good reasons for the Viper's bargain-basement $62K tariff. No roof, for instance. And a hose-it-down plasticky interior with low-rent switchgear. And a ride like a Ford F150's. And a full-throttle exhaust blat that sounds like a tornado ripping out the seams of a Holy Rollers' revival tent. All of which we graciously accept, because it's precisely what Chrysler promised back in 1992. What we *didn't* count on was this car's spooky steering and villainous handling.

The Viper hunts and darts under braking. It resolutely follows even minute irregularities in the road. Its rear end steps out when you poke the power. And, as Csaba Csere describes it: "There's a moment where *nothing* happens between turn-in and when the tires actually hook up. It saps your confidence if you're hustling."

The snaky handling ("This is the only car I've ever spun on the skidpad," notes Don Schroeder) is likely a result of unfinished development. God knows, the Viper has all the rubber it could ever want, and its weight bias is the closest to perfect in this group—an astounding claim for a car whose nose carries an engine the size of John Madden's refrigerator.

In many ways, owning a Viper is like owning a powerful motorcycle. "Without a real top, it's too reliant on the weather," says Kevin Smith, who also noted that removing and replacing those rudimentary canvas pieces is a tedious, fussy, two-man job. "Yeah, it's the world's largest Fat Boy Harley," added Yates, "and you might even want to put your feet down roaring into turns—this is the only non-ABS-equipped car in the bunch." Also the only one without even a single airbag.

Although it's tied with the 911 Turbo in the horsepower wars, the Viper accelerates to 60 mph and through the quarter-mile half a second slower. Put 400 horsepower in nearly any street car and you might want to think about four-wheel drive, a concept that was implemented in Weissach but not at the New Mack Assembly Plant.

The Viper is like using a Louisville Slugger to play ping-pong. You wind up with drastic, if clumsy, results. It is big, crude, deafening, and something of a cartoon. "On the other hand," noted Yates in the logbook, "every time we'd show up in a small town, the locals clumped around one car and one car *only*: the one built in Detroit."

Third Place
Ferrari F355

For Ferrari, the F355 is a radical departure. Don't believe us? Consider one entry in its logbook: "This car has a climate-control system that really works; in fact, it works better than the Porsche's."

C/D has traditionally been slow to praise Ferraris, in part because the manufacturer's performance claims tend to be inflated, in part because the cars have been impractical and unreliable, in part because their sticker prices gave us nosebleeds.

So check out the stats on the company's newest and

FERRARI F355

Highs: Flexible and symphonic V-8, limpet-like grip; the status slaves' hall-of-famer.

Lows: Fifties-vintage shifter, stratospheric price; talk to your insurance agent.

The Verdict: Maranello's best-ever all-around sports car. No bull.

C/D Test Results

			accleration, sec								
	0–30 mph	0–60 mph	0–100 mph	0–130 mph	0–150 mph	1/4-mile	street start, 5–60 mph	top gear, 30–50 mph	top gear, 50–70 mph	top speed, mph	braking, 70–0 mph, ft
ACURA NSX-T	1.9	5.2	13.0	24.7	45.5	13.8 @ 103 mph	5.7	7.3	7.3	162	173
DODGE VIPER RT/10	1.7	4.3	10.5	19.0	38.3	12.8 @ 109 mph	5.0	9.7	10.8	168	180
FERRARI F355	1.8	4.5	10.9	19.1	28.7	13.0 @ 110 mph	5.6	8.1	8.5	179	165
LOTUS ESPRIT S4S	1.6	4.4	10.9	20.1	40.0	13.0 @ 108 mph	6.0	13.1	7.4	162	189
PORSCHE 911 TURBO	1.3	3.7	9.4	17.1	20.5	12.3 @ 114 mph	4.5	9.7	7.5	176	162
TEST AVERAGE	1.7	4.4	10.9	20.0	34.6	13.0 @ 109 mph	5.4	9.6	8.3	169	174

Vital Statistics

	price, base/ as tested	engine	SAE net power/torque	transmission/ gear ratios:1/ maximum test speed, mph/ axle ratio:1	curb weight, lb	weight distribution, % F/R
ACURA NSX-T	$86,642/ $86,642	DOHC 24-valve V-6, 182 cu in (2977cc), aluminum block and heads, Honda PGM-FI engine-control system with port fuel injection	270 bhp @ 7100 rpm/ 210 lb-ft @ 5300 rpm	5-speed/ 3.07, 1.80, 1.23, 0.97, 0.77/ 46, 86, 115, 146, 162/ 4.06, limited slip	3110	42.1/57.9
DODGE VIPER RT/10	$61,975/ $61,975	pushrod 20-valve V-10, 488 cu in (7990cc), aluminum block and heads, Chrysler engine-control system with port fuel injection	400 bhp @ 4600 rpm/ 465 lb-ft @ 3600 rpm	6-speed/ 2.66, 1.78, 1.30, 1.00, 0.74, 0.50/ 55, 83, 113, 147, 168, 155/ 3.07, limited slip	3534	50.9/49.1
FERRARI F355	$128,800/ $128,800	DOHC 40-valve V-8, 213 cu in (3496cc), aluminum block and heads, Bosch Motronic 2.7 engine-control system with port fuel injection	375 bhp @ 8250 rpm/ 268 lb-ft @ 6000 rpm	6-speed/ 3.06, 2.16, 1.61, 1.27, 1.03, 0.84/ 49, 69, 93, 118, 145, 179/ 3.56, limited slip	3270	42.0/58.0
LOTUS ESPRIT S4S	$80,340/ $87,904	turbocharged and intercooled DOHC 16-valve 4-in-line, 133 cu in (2174cc), aluminum block and head, Lotus-GM engine-control system with port fuel injection	300 bhp @ 6400 rpm/ 277 lb-ft @ 4100 rpm	5-speed/ 3.36, 2.06, 1.38, 1.04, 0.82/ 41, 66, 99, 132, 162/ 3.89	2969	44.5/55.5
PORSCHE 911 TURBO	$106,465/ $106,465	twin-turbocharged and intercooled SOHC 12-valve flat 6, 220 cu in (3600cc), aluminum block and heads, Bosch Motronic 5.2 engine-control system with port fuel injection	400 bhp @ 5750 rpm/ 400 lb-ft @ 4500 rpm	6-speed/ 3.82, 2.15, 1.56, 1.21, 0.97, 0.75/ 36, 63, 87, 113, 140, 176/ 3.44, limited slip	3362	38.9/61.1

cheapest offering: 0-to-60 and quarter-mile times only 0.2 second behind the 400-hp Viper's. A stopping distance so close to the Porsche's that Stuttgart's engineers may pull a full Jonestown Kool-Aid klatch. And skidpad grip that, at *1.02 g,* not only surpasses everything in this comparo but also bests the company's own street-legal racer, the F40.

Add to that terrific steering with power assist as nearly perfect as the NSX's, not to mention better visibility. Plus a ride that is taut without becoming harsh, not what you'd expect from a one-g suspension. Plus an 8500-rpm redline that produces an engine howl so sonorous, so much like a lightly muffled F1 car, that the driver doesn't really miss the optional radio. (Hey, you want *every*thing for only $128,800?)

"In the details of this car, Ferrari has done a lot of what Acura did to define itself, way back when," wrote Kevin

Smith. Indeed, the F355 offers adjustable shocks, unique in this group. It has firm seats that can be twisted into a wide variety of supportive shapes, plus a sophisticated exhaust bypass that meets emissions regs without strangling the 375-horse V-8.

Although it's on such a clear course to modernizing its cars, Maranello ought to continue improving them. The gated, metallic shifter is still a chore and a gratuitous anachronism. The steering wheel, although adjustable, gives you the choice of either a good driving position or viewing the instruments, but not both. Moreover, this is the second F355 we've tested whose sticky throttle made it impossible to pick up the power smoothly in mid-corner. And this engine's 24 inlet valves are so deft at swallowing accelerants that the F355's cruising range (when the fuel light began to glow) averaged just under 200 miles. (Yes, we were driving like Gerhard Berger, though not as neatly. But fuel economy *worse* than a 488-cubic-inch Viper? Don't tell the Vatican.)

Only two points out of second place, the Ferrari was the Big Surprise in this comparo. "If the thing just cost a little less—say, the same as the Porsche," noted Kevin Smith, "it would easily have been in second place. In fact, I might have voted it the winner."

Second Place
Acura NSX-T

For the last five years, we've regularly gushed and spouted and pontificated about the essential goodness, the quintessential purity, of Acura's NSX. So don't be shocked that this, the least powerful car in our super five (and also the slowest to 60 mph and through the quarter-mile), finished only three points behind the fastest, most powerful car in the group.

How can this happen? Here's how: track numbers tell you zip about a car's usable performance in Ann Arbor traffic,

roadholding, 300-ft skidpad, g	emergency lane change, mph	interior sound level, dBA				fuel economy, mpg		
		idle	full throttle	70-mph cruising	70-mph coasting	EPA city	EPA highway	C/D 950-mile trip
0.95	63.4	49	89	78	78	18	24	18
0.98	61.9	66	86	81	81	14	22	14
1.02	67.2	69	84	76	76	10	15	13
0.94	70.9	58	80	76	76	17	27	17
0.95	69.8	56	81	76	75	13	19	14
0.97	*66.6*	*60*	*84*	*77*	*77*	*14*	*21*	*15*

dimensions, in				fuel tank, gal	interior volume, cu ft		suspension		brakes, F/R	tires
wheel-base	length	width	height		front	trunk	front	rear		
99.6	174.2	71.3	46.1	18.5	49	5	ind, unequal-length control arms, coil springs, anti-roll bar	ind, unequal-length control arms and a toe-control link, coil springs, anti-roll bar	vented disc/ vented disc; anti-lock control	Yokohama A-022; F: 215/45ZR-16, R: 245/40ZR-17
96.2	175.1	75.7	44.0	22.0	48	5	ind, unequal-length control arms, coil springs, anti-roll bar	ind, unequal-length control arms and a toe-control link, coil springs, anti-roll bar	vented disc/ vented disc	Michelin XGT Z; F: P275/40ZR-17, R: P335/35ZR-17
96.5	167.3	74.8	46.1	21.7	47	8	ind, unequal-length control arms, coil springs, 2-position cockpit-adjustable electronically controlled shock absorbers, anti-roll bar	ind, unequal-length control arms, coil springs, 2-position cockpit-adjustable electronically controlled shock absorbers, anti-roll bar	vented disc/ vented disc; anti-lock control	Pirelli PZero Asimmetrico; F: 225/40ZR-18, R: 265/40ZR-18
96.0	172.0	73.5	45.3	19.3	47	8	ind, unequal-length control arms, coil springs, anti-roll bar	ind, 1 trailing arm and 2 lateral links per side, coil springs	vented disc/ vented disc; anti-lock control	Goodyear Eagle GS-A; F: 215/40ZR-17, R: 245/45ZR-17
89.4	167.7	70.7	51.8	19.4	43	3	ind, strut located by a control arm, coil springs, anti-roll bar	ind; lower control arm with 1 lateral link, 1 diagonal link, and 2 toe-control links per side; coil springs; anti-roll bar	vented, drilled disc/ vented, drilled disc; anti-lock control	Pirelli PZero Asimmetrico; F: 225/40ZR-18, R: 285/30ZR-18

THE SUPERCAR OLYMPICS

ACURA NSX-T

Highs: Surgical steering, magical shifter, seats that satisfy all known anatomies.

Lows: Near-stark interior, some mundane-looking switchgear, but that's about it.

The Verdict: A comfortable 162-mph slot car available for everyday use.

and they tell you little about making nine-tenths passes on the blind, downhill, off-camber turn just outside Burr Oak Lodge.

The Acura NSX is as user-friendly as the tumblers on a Mosler vault. Check out the expansive view from its low, forward cockpit. Try finding a clutch and shifter combo that so telepathically slides gears into place. See if you can locate *any* seats that are both this comfortable and this adept at distributing side forces. Locate a steering rack that delivers this much feedback sans kickback. Identify a removable targa top that can be stowed onboard without reducing cargo-carrying capacity by one cubic inch.

Built with the same monumental attention to ergonomic detail as a Honda Accord, the NSX sometimes takes a knock or two for being *too* familiar, at least inside, where some of the switchgear is pedestrian and the cockpit is an unnecessarily dour arena in which to celebrate so much fun underfoot. On this trip—for the first time—editors fantasized openly, if not vociferously, about obtaining more power, especially when the car was asked to

launch itself out of tight uphill esses and switchbacks. One editor suggested a supercharger, another wanted a 3.0-liter V-8, a third asked whether a streetable version of Honda's racing V-10 might fit. Which, in turn, made us wonder whether a six-speed gearbox, rather than the mandatory five, might also make life easier.

At $86,642, the NSX is no longer the striking bargain it was 60 months ago. Still, where the Viper offers a huge bang for the buck, the NSX is big civil subtlety for the buck. This is the brain surgeon's approach to go-fast operations. From its bird-bones suspension bits to its lacy aluminum skin, the NSX delivers supercar precision without beating up its owner.

But beware: Although you can throw it around; you can also throw it away.

First Place
Porsche 911 Turbo

It's the kind of formula you'd concoct in high-school study hall. Take a chassis *four inches* shorter than a Jeep Wrangler's, then install a twin-turbo engine with, say, *400* horsepower hung way the hell behind the rear wheels. The result

PORSCHE 911 TURBO

Highs: Sumptuous luxo amenities, effortless velocity, astounding brakes.

Lows: Feathery steering, gimcrack security system, shifter that can confuse.

The Verdict: Ear-pinning performance, probably the planet's most practical supercar.

THE SUPERCAR OLYMPICS

should be something akin to a golf cart powered by two General Electric turbines—the sort of car that would crash as you backed it out of your driveway.

Instead, the outcome is the most obscenely fast and sophisticated Porsche since Weissach loosed upon civilized society the all-wheel-drive 959 nine years ago. The new 911 Turbo is our choice as this planet's most eminently practical supercar, the quickest A-to-B four-wheeled transport to alight on American highways.

About now, you're probably muttering, "What about the Ferrari F40 or Lamborghini Diablo VT?" Forget 'em. If you've got 3.7 seconds to spare, the 911 Turbo will hand you 60 mph. That leaves the F40 half a second in the dust. Or, if you've got some empty road near your house, this Porsche will swallow 1320 feet of it 1.7 seconds sooner than your neighbor's Lamborghini Diablo VT.

Not that those comparisons mean much anyway. The nervous F40 and the fat Diablo are 30-minute cars. After that, you'd like a cool drink and a brief nap. Not so the 911 Turbo. Cruising around town, this Porsche is more docile than a Carrera 2, partly because it's quieter and partly because the standard luxo bits inside are more posh. And when you finally *do* tip into the KKK turbos, there's no tire squeal, no exhaust roar, no darty nose. Just a seamless, silent, drama-free delivery of endless torque, accompanied by a rush of scenery that within two or three seconds takes on a vaguely hallucinatory hue, as if the nearby trees were all recently vandalized by Matisse.

"Twice on brief straightaways," noted one editor in the Turbo's logbook, "I glanced down and discovered I had innocently dialed up 130 mph. I'd have been horrified if I hadn't had Porsche's brakes beneath me."

Not quite matching this machine's warp-drive potential for effortless velocity are the clutch and steering—one is uncommunicative, the other is simply too light. Porsche intentionally removed 25 percent of the clutch-pedal effort, plus 15 percent of its travel. And as for the feathery steering, well, maybe it's those new 8-by-18-inch front wheels or the GT2's racing power-assist. Whatever the reason, the more rudimentary Carrera 2's steering remains the best sports rack in the world, and we wish the engineers hadn't messed with it.

Ditto the Turbo's security system. An ignition bypass is triggered by pressing a button on the key fob. It sounds simple enough, but you can't imagine the driver's fury when he inserts the key, twists it for liftoff, and absolutely nothing happens. Can you say "gimcrackery"?

We dubbed the Porsche "the lazy man's supercar," at least on the roads of southern Ohio. Although the Turbo is the second-heaviest car in this quintet, Porsche has pretty well masked its traditional tail-wagging-the-dog handling. Give our drivers 400 horsepower plus astounding wet-weather grip and they will—using one hand and half a head of concentration—keep up with *any* other supercar in this group. "It's almost like cheating," wrote Kevin Smith.

We'll come back to this wonderment, in part to report more definitively on some un-Teutonic assembly glitches. Our test car suffered an inoperative "Litronic" low-beam lamp, a snapped-off hood latch, a sunroof that ate fuses like popcorn, and a glovebox that randomly flopped open and spilled its considerable guts.

Still, no piece of machinery producing 400 horses has any right to feel so tame and violence-free. Said one editor, "I can't explain it, unless this car is powered by dilithium crystals." The new Porsche 911 Turbo is the German engineers' 176-mph answer to whatever the question was, or will be. Captain Swiggett should be told. •

Editors' Ratings

	engine	transmission	brakes	handling	ride	comfort	ergonomics	fit and finish	value	styling	fun to drive	shock factor	OVERALL RATING*
ACURA NSX-T	9	10	8	9	9	10	10	10	9	8	9	7	**93**
DODGE VIPER RT/10	8	8	8	7	7	7	7	6	7	9	7	10	**83**
FERRARI F355	10	7	9	9	8	8	7	8	7	9	10	9	**91**
LOTUS ESPRIT S4S	7	6	7	8	8	6	6	7	6	8	8	7	**81**
PORSCHE 911 TURBO	10	8	10	9	9	9	8	9	9	8	9	7	**96**

HOW IT WORKS: Editors rate vehicles from 1 to 10 (10 being best) in each category, then scores are collected and averaged, resulting in the numbers shown above.

*The Overall Rating is not the total of those numbers. Rather, it is an independent judgment (on a 1-to-100 scale) that includes other factors—even personal preferences—not easily categorized.

Dodge
VIPER RT/10

For 1996, this snake charmer packs a more venomous punch

BY DOUGLAS KOTT
PHOTOS BY JOHN LAMM

NEVER MIND THAT on a sunny day in Los Angeles the Viper's interior smells of hot composites, baked unrelentingly by close-fitting exhaust pipes routed under the doors' thick sills. Disregard the sound of the engine at idle—a wheezy, chirpy throb that you'd sooner associate with a UPS delivery truck than with a 170-mph sports car. And pay no attention to the heavy clutch and slow-speed driveline clumsiness that'll make the smuggest of parking valets look like a first-week Driver's Ed student.

So when other cars were getting their diplomas from finishing school, the Viper was out dodging the truancy officer. But like any street-smart kid, it made up for its lack of polish in ways no other car could ever hope to emulate. The Viper is all about elemental thrills; explosive power delivered with above-average precision; Muscle-Beach, broad-shouldered looks with the goods to back up the implied challenge. With the first unbridled blast down a two-lane road, its irritations seem minor and petty—it's like saying, "Yeah, that Cindy Crawford's a real looker, but there *is* that mole above her lip."

Case in point: Crack open the twin throttle bodies with your right foot, and the sort of thrust known previously to astronauts, fighter jocks and human cannonballs is yours. The enormous 8.0-liter pushrod V-10 might seem crude in mechanical specification, but its execution is first-class—a steel-sleeved aluminum block developed with the help of Lamborghini, forged connecting rods and crankshaft, and a mild camshaft with minimal overlap for docile low-rev operation. New this year are a revised windage tray that helps prevent the crank from whipping the oil into froth and a rear-exit exhaust system that provides meaningful gains in horsepower (to 415, up 15) and torque (to 488 lb.-ft., up 33).

With such monstrous outputs to begin with, these changes register more with our road test equipment than through the seat of our pants. The Viper is quicker than the 1995 model and, believe you me, can out-thunder almost anything short of a 12-cylinder Italian exotic or Porsche 911 Turbo through the quarter mile. How about 12.9 seconds past the timing lights? Or 4.6 sec. to 60 mph? The Ferrari F40 and Vector W8, each orders of magnitude more expensive, are the only rear-drive production cars listed in our Road Test Summary that can trounce it. And beyond the numbers, the Viper simply takes charge of the drag strip, with mechanical war whoops issuing from beneath the enormous clamshell hood, unlike, say, the whisper-jet thrust of that supercar from Zuffenhausen. As each shift is grabbed, the 335-section Michelins claw at the asphalt and vault the Viper into another glorious orgy of acceleration, seemingly as forceful as the previous one. When its engine is on full boil, there is something so utterly *unstoppable* about this car; a backroom deal seems to have been made to bend the laws of physics here.

The sounds are better too, thanks to the rear-exit exhaust, a happy byproduct of the GTS Coupe's development. Drivers of earlier sidepipe Vipers put up with the hiss of wildly rushing air pouring out the aft ends of the rocker panels. But with the new system, routed as before through the sills but making an inward turn up and over the rear

100

■ Viper's absence of body roll and double-bubble detachable hardtop can be seen clearly here. Clamshell bonnet gets whimsical snake badge. Overhead-valve V-10 powerhouse has significant horsepower and torque gains through a less restrictive exhaust system.

THE COMPETITION

Chevrolet Corvette LT1

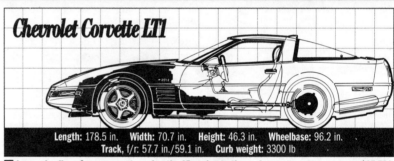

Length: 178.5 in. Width: 70.7 in. Height: 46.3 in. Wheelbase: 96.2 in.
Track, f/r: 57.7 in./59.1 in. Curb weight: 3300 lb

■ In nearly all performance categories the Viper beats the Vette. The exception is in braking, where the Vette's standard ABS facilitates stops that are shorter than the Viper's. Both Viper and Vette are potent roadsters, but the Corvette has an edge in refinement, making it an easier everyday car. The only way to get a Convertible with a manual gearbox is to order the new LT4 engine, which has 330 bhp. The 300-bhp LT1 is offered only with an automatic. The performance numbers at right are from a Corvette coupe. *(Tested: 2/94)*

Current list price............ **$37,790**
Engine.............. ohv 5.7-liter **V-8**
Horsepower .. **300 bhp @ 5000 rpm**
Torque....... **335 lb-ft @ 3600 rpm**
Transmission .... **6-speed manual**
0–60 mph.................. **5.7 sec**
Braking, 60–0 mph.......... **123 ft**
Lateral accel (200-ft skidpad): **0.87g**
EPA city/highway .... **17/25 mpg**

Mitsubishi 3000GT Spyder VR-4

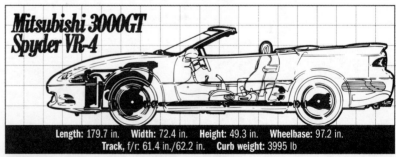

Length: 179.7 in. Width: 72.4 in. Height: 49.3 in. Wheelbase: 97.2 in.
Track, f/r: 61.4 in./62.2 in. Curb weight: 3995 lb

■ With its one-button retractable hardtop, the 3000GT Spyder boasts the most unusual roof since Ford's Skyliner back in the Fifties. At nearly 4000 lb., the Spyder is by no means a lightweight, but it packs a 320-bhp V-6 under its wide hood that makes 60 mph arrive in a scant 5.4 seconds. This 4-cam, twin-turbo V-6 doesn't boast the low-end hit of the Viper, but its on-boost powerband is especially wide. A 2+2, the Spyder can carry four if the need arises, but it's really best for two people and luggage. *(Tested: 8/95)*

Current list price **$64,449**
Engine .. twin-turbo dohc 3.0-liter **V-6**
Horsepower .. **320 bhp @ 6000 rpm**
Torque....... **315 lb-ft @ 2500 rpm**
Transmission .... **6-speed manual**
0–60 mph.................. **5.4 sec**
Braking, 60–0 mph.......... **132 ft**
Lateral accel (200-ft skidpad): **0.88g**
EPA city/highway .... **18/24 mpg**

suspension to a tandem muffler and twin center-mounted outlets, the Viper finally has a respectable exhaust note. While it's not the chunky, musical burble of a V-8—the V-10's note is slightly reedier, less mellifluous—it's a huge improvement, right down to the slight *phapp phapp phapp* backfires echoing through the system on the overrun. Glorious! Now if only something could be done about that idle.

Peer into a wheel well, past enormous Brembo brake calipers and 13.0-in. rotors, and more GTS Coupe hand-me-downs can be seen. The welded-up tubular A-arms are gone, replaced with ones cast of high-ductility A206 aluminum alloy. These, along with steering knuckles and rear hub carriers made of a like material plus hollow anti-roll bars, are good for a 15-lb.-per-corner savings. Add this compliance-enhancing improvement to revisions in the rear suspension geometry (increased caster angle, lower roll center, reduced lateral movement through the suspension's stroke) and you have, in theory, a less tempestuous snake.

The Viper has never been a paragon

1996 Dodge VIPER RT/10

MANUFACTURER
Chrysler Corporation
12000 Chrysler Dr.
Highland Park, Mich. 48288

PRICE
List price	$58,500
Price as tested	$68,850

Price as tested includes std equip. (folding soft top with side curtains, 6-speaker AM/FM-cassette sound system, alarm system, leather upholstery), air cond ($1200), removable hardtop with sliding side curtains ($2500), luxury tax ($3350), gas-guzzler tax ($2600), dest charge ($700).

0–60 mph	4.6 sec
0–¼ mi	12.9 sec
Top speed	est 170 mph
Skidpad	0.96g
Slalom	62.0 mph
Brake rating	excellent

TEST CONDITIONS
Temperature	85° F
Wind	calm
Humidity	na
Elevation	990 ft

SCALE: 10 in. (254mm) DIVISIONS
DRAWING BY BILL DOBSON

ENGINE
Type.. **aluminum block and heads, V-10**
Valvetrain.............. ohv 2 valve/cyl
Displacement...... 488 cu in./7990 cc
Bore x stroke....... 4.00 x 3.88 in./
101.6 x 98.5 mm
Compression ratio............ 9.1:1
Horsepower
(SAE)....... **415 bhp @ 5200 rpm**
Bhp/liter.................... 51.9
Torque........ **488 lb-ft @ 3600 rpm**
Maximum engine speed.... 6000 rpm
Fuel injection.... elect. sequential port
Fuel.... prem unleaded, 91 pump oct

CHASSIS & BODY
Layout....... **front engine/rear drive**
Body/frame.... **resin transfer molded composite/tubular steel**
Brakes
Front...... **13.0-in. vented discs**
Rear....... **13.0-in. vented discs**
Assist type................. vacuum
Total swept area........ 254 sq in.
Swept area/ton........ 141 sq in.
Wheels................. forged alloy;
17 x 10 f, 17 x 13 r
Tires........... Michelin Pilot MXX3;
P275/40ZR-17 f, P335/35ZR-17 r
Steering... **rack & pinion,** power assist
Overall ratio.............. 16.7:1
Turns, lock to lock........... 2.4
Turning circle............. 40.5 ft
Suspension
Front....... **unequal-length A-arms,** coil springs, tube shocks, anti-roll bar
Rear....... **unequal-length A-arms, toe-control links,** coil springs, tube shocks, anti-roll bar

DRIVETRAIN
Transmission... 6-sp manual

Gear	Ratio	Overall ratio	(Rpm)	Mph
1st	2.66:1	8.17:1	(6000)	54
2nd	1.78:1	5.46:1	(6000)	81
3rd	1.30:1	3.99:1	(6000)	111
4th	1.00:1	3.07:1	(6000)	144
5th	0.74:1	2.27:1	est (4960)	170
6th	0.50:1	1.54:1	est (3970)	170

Final drive ratio... 3.07:1
Engine rpm @ 60 mph in 6th............................... 1400

GENERAL DATA
Curb weight............ **3440 lb**
Test weight............. 3590 lb
Weight dist (with driver), f/r, %........ 49/51
Wheelbase............. 96.2 in.
Track, f/r..... 59.6 in./60.6 in.
Length................. **175.1 in.**
Width.................. **75.7 in.**
Height................. **43.9 in.**
Ground clearance........ 5.0 in.
Trunk space........... 6.5 cu ft

MAINTENANCE
Oil/filter change.... 3000 mi/3000 mi
Tuneup................ 30,000 mi
Basic warranty..... 3 years/36,000 mi

ACCOMMODATIONS
Seating capacity............... 2
Head room................... na
Seat width.......... 2 x 18.5 in.
Leg room................ 44.5 in.
Seat travel............... 6.0 in.

INTERIOR NOISE
Idle in neutral.............. 70 dBA
Maximum in 1st gear....... 87 dBA
Constant 50 mph........... 79 dBA
70 mph................. 84 dBA

INSTRUMENTATION
180-mph speedometer, 7000-rpm tach, coolant temp, oil press., fuel level, volts

ACCELERATION
Time to speed	Seconds
0–30 mph	1.8
0–40 mph	2.5
0–50 mph	3.3
0–60 mph	4.6
0–70 mph	5.6
0–80 mph	6.9
0–90 mph	8.9
0–100 mph	10.5

Time to distance
0–100 ft................ 2.8
0–500 ft................ 7.1
0–1320 ft (¼ mi): 12.9 @ 112.0 mph

FUEL ECONOMY
Normal driving........... 13.9 mpg
EPA city/highway........ 12/21 mpg
Cruise range............ 250 miles
Fuel capacity........... 19.0 gal.

BRAKING
Minimum stopping distance
From 60 mph............. 136 ft
From 80 mph............. 232 ft
Control.................. excellent
Pedal effort for 0.5g stop...... 17 lb
Fade, effort after six 0.5g stops from 60 mph.................... 17 lb
Brake feel.............. very good
Overall brake rating........ excellent

HANDLING
Lateral accel (200-ft skidpad)... 0.96g
Balance............ mild understeer
Speed thru 700-ft slalom.... 62.0 mph
Balance............ mild understeer
Lateral seat support....... excellent

Subjective ratings consist of excellent, very good, good, average, poor; na means information is not available.

Test Notes...

■ With 488 lb-ft of torque beneath your right foot, the Viper requires finesse for a smooth drag-strip launch. Too many revs and the result is hopeless wheelspin. Wheel hop, however, is held to a bare minimum.

■ Despite the Viper's imposing width and not-inconsiderable weight, it threads through the slalom with surprising nimbleness. Though the tail drifts slightly, it's easily caught with a flick of steering.

■ Decibel levels at idle and 70 mph aren't much different from the last Viper we tested, but the sound quality has certainly improved—thanks to a new exhaust that merges two banks of five cylinders.

■ Enormous center console, body-gripping seats, hooded main dials and electric-red leather accents set off the Viper's interior. Below, stronger-than-coffee yellow wheels. At bottom, notice centered exhaust tips, finished in polished ceramic.

of stability—any time you couple a short wheelbase, quick steering and the sort of torque figures usually reserved for Caterpillar earth-movers, the result can be twitchiness at the edge of adhesion and difficult recovery (it's a heavy car, estimated at 3440 lb.) past that edge. But changes here have charmed the snake, lending a more agile feel and causing less apprehension as the limit is approached. Cornering is so flat and tires are so quiet that you'd almost welcome more roll and squeal. But if you patiently work to the edge of the envelope, the big Dodge rewards with precision, sure-footedness and 0.96g of seat bolster-compressing grip. And with so much straightaway-shortening power on tap, you never feel the need to really late-brake the entrance of a turn.

Should you need the brakes, they're as reassuring as your father's hand on your shoulder. Pedal feel is firm, the bite of the aluminum 4-piston front calipers is instantaneous without being grabby, and stopping distances are admirably short. It seems odd to have such a powerful car without ABS (as I was reminded when I repeatedly locked a right-front wheel at a silty photo-shoot turnaround point), but it's no great loss as the brakes are wonderfully easy to modulate.

With the beast tamed (or at least calmed) in the handling department, the Viper Team turned toward creature comforts. Not that they'd do anything to take away from the Viper's basic, brutish nature, but the improvements—an optional $2500 removable

hardtop and side curtains—are welcome. Secured with convertible-type twist latches in front and Allen caphead screws in the back, the top has a subtle double-bubble shape (no doubt inspired by numerous Zagato designs) that lends the interior vast amounts of head room. Side curtains for this top fit quite snugly and have panes of rigid clear plastic that slide back for access to the interior door releases (remember, there are no external door handles to distract from the Viper's powerful lines). Of course, a folding fabric top and side curtains with zippered flexible vinyl windows are standard equipment, but once you've experienced the improved sealing and neater appearance of the optional setup, there's just no turning back.

The final changes to the 1996 Viper are cosmetic and are, uh, bold. One of us dubbed this particular paint treatment the "catsup-and-mustard car," but you have the option of American racing colors (white with blue stripes, with white painted wheels) or black with silver stripes, with polished wheels. You didn't think the Viper could be any less subtle? Think again! Our test car's interior was equally vivid with bright leather covering the steering wheel, shift knob and parking-brake grip, in a shade I call "Carol Channing Lipstick Red." You can almost see it with your eyes closed.

The world is overrun with timid, practical cars, driven by people who don't necessarily want to be noticed. Drive a Viper, and you *will* be noticed. Kids, adults, housewives, the elderly will come over to look, and you'll be obliged to answer questions to the point of hoarseness. But it's a good kind of hoarse, chatting about a most exceptional snake.

ROAD TEST

Dodge Viper RT/10

Chrysler says changes for 1996 transform this now five-year-old sinner. We say, "Show us."

BY PATRICK BEDARD

The Viper is the New Chrysler Corporation's attempt at atonement, at making up for the sins it committed against cars—all those bogus wire wheel covers and limp shock absorbers and padded-vinyl roofs—during the reign of Lee the Imperious. And by the precise calculations of our test department, each Viper built since the 1992 intro cancels out 817 K-car New Yorkers.

A lot of "nice" Chryslers were inflicted on the market in those years (more than it could stand, in fact), but the Viper goes about the work of offsetting them with a swaggering gusto. There's not a nice fiber in its glass body. It's so ornery it won't even cancel its own turn signals. "Knife-in-the-back handling" we said in our last test ("The Supercar Olympics," July 1995). "Big, crude, deafening, and something of a cartoon," we said. "Villainous." (We don't hold back once we get the adjectives flowing.)

Now we learn that particular Viper was having a bad suspension day—month, actually—during our last test. Wheel alignment was way wrong. High-grip tires don't like being pointed in contradictory directions. For the record, when we phoned Chrysler *before* the test to say the suspension had passed through independent and was well on its way to defiant, we were told: "They're all like that."

Anyway, that was then and this is 1996 and the Viper has undergone, for the new year, its first change of underwear since its 1992 introduction. It has a new frame, new suspension, new tires and, what it really needed all along, more horsepower. Surely the New Yorker cancellation rate will be much enhanced by such extensive reengineering. Knowing how you care about such things, we set up an all-Viper comparison—the exact same test car of last summer, fresh from alignment therapy, versus a pre-production 1996 model.

It's easy to spot the model-year differences on the outside. There are no side exhausts on the new car, racing stripes now appear on both white and black cars, and wheels are different—they're painted an astonishing yellow on red cars. Inside, the black cockpits are spiced up with vividly colored leather on the wheel rim, shift knob, and brake handle—it's bright blue on white cars, lipstick-red on red cars. "I won't go into the politics on that," said engineer Pete Gladysz, who is chassis and design manager on the Viper Project.

From the driver's seat, it's easy to spot differences, too. The new car's ride is less punishing, the cockpit is much quieter now that exhaust goes out behind, the steering doesn't squirm as much on truck-worn pavement, and the brake feel is more conventional—it's very good too, thanks to

PHOTOGRAPHY BY AARON KILEY

THE VERDICT

Highs: The way other cars let you go first, prodigious g-forces, sunny days.

Lows: Interior hospitality of a grizzly's den, assembly details that look homemade, rainy days.

The Verdict: A raw-meat roadster for the guy who doesn't care what anybody says.

Chrysler ending its infatuation with a quirky booster that gave remarkably short pedal travel instead of good modulation. "We thought it felt like a Ferrari F40," Gladysz explains.

Gladysz says most of the 1996 changes were made in anticipation of future model needs and to comply with regulations. The first of the future models is the coupe, due in late spring. Inevitably, it will be heavier. So the engineers went looking for offsetting weight reductions to build into the basic car, and they found enough to lighten the roadster by 90 pounds (our test car, a prototype, is about 60 pounds overweight). Logically, the less drafty, less leaky coupe will encourage driving on colder, wetter days, so new tires were sought. "I didn't say all-weather tires," Gladysz reminds.

On the regulatory side, lower noise standards are coming in Europe, and new emissions requirements are coming in the U.S., occasioned by the on-board diagnostics OBD II rule (see page 87). For both noise and OBD II, the side exhausts had to go. Everybody wins: the new system pipes the noise far behind the cockpit and away from the occupants' ears, and it improves the exhaust note while reducing back-

pressure. Output rises 15 hp as a result.

Weight reduction also brings gains. The frame loses 60 pounds while improving 20 percent in torsional stiffness. New suspension arms and knuckles are now aluminum, and the wheels are slightly lighter. Together, those changes reduce unsprung weight substantially. Front-suspension geometry remains as before, but the rear roll center was lowered to reduce tire scrub—to cut down on self-steering in the truck ruts. At both ends, shocks are new and their attachments were moved closer to the lower ball joints for better control of small suspension movements.

Powertrain changes are numerous as well. Cooling-system capacity is increased, and the clutch, differential, and half-shafts have been upsized for more torque (Gladysz alludes to a future need for this extra beef, without confirming the limited run of high-output Vipers we expect in time for racing season). A power-steering cooler was added.

Tire sizes remain as before, but the carcass construction, tread pattern, and compound reflect an entirely different approach to performance in these new-to-the-U.S. Pilot SX Michelins. Contrary to Gladysz's prediction, we find them slightly less grippy on the skidpad than the Michelin XGT Z tires of the 1995 car on hand for comparison: 0.97 g versus 1.00 g. They seem to understeer more, too—for sure, they require larger steering angles at any given lateral force. And they make a shrill howl at the limit.

That's the bad news. The good news is that the car behaves better on them in every other way. Along with the suspension changes, they vastly improve handling. When cornering at the limit, the new Viper no longer seems balanced on a knife edge. It's more gradual. The tail now slips into a drift angle. Even with alignment properly set, the 1995 car is still snappish—it'll bite if you change power or steering imprudently near the limit. The new version is far more tolerant. You can work with it, make corrections, adjust your path, even as you approach the hairy edge. Proof of this new attitude shows up during hot laps. At the Chrysler proving grounds

DODGE VIPER RT/10

roadcourse, our man Don Schroeder drove a six-lap session in each car. His best time in the '96 was 1:17.47, with a best-lap-to-worst-lap variation of only 0.08 second. In the old car, he managed one lap in 1:17.32, but the best-to-worst variation exceeded two seconds and cumulative time was far behind.

Chrysler showed us a naked mule (below), pointing out new suspension pieces and new shock placement. Frame loses 60 pounds but gains torsional stiffness.

Heard from trackside, the 1995 exhaust at full power hisses like a shot-down blimp, seriously uncool compared with the disciplined roar of the new one.

On the road, the difference between new and old is no less dramatic. Tire noise on textured roads used to be deafening; now it's merely excessive (like everything else about the Viper). Ride is much improved too, enough for us to upgrade our rating from the previous "terrible" to "bad." Perhaps because of the additional frame stiffness, the body is less clattery.

Gladysz says the new tires are significantly better in braking. Certainly they team happily with the new booster to shorten stopping distances from 177 feet in the realigned '95 car to 163 feet. Pedal feel is much better too, which is particularly important because the Viper does not offer ABS.

The Viper's bountiful torque "flat"— the curve, like Nebraska, is flat as far as the eye can see—gives a peculiarly constant acceleration, sort of a civilian substitute for a Saturn booster. The extra 15 advertised horses were definitely on the job the day we tested the two cars back-to-back—0 to 60 mph improves by a tenth of a second to 4.1 seconds, the quarter-mile quickens by a tenth of a second and 1 mph to 12.6 seconds at 113 mph, and top speed rises to 173 mph from 167. A down-to-weight production car should be slightly quicker.

While the changes for 1996 add up to a more powerful and less belligerent machine, the Viper remains outrageous by intent: the cockpit smells like fiberglass, and its weather protection stows in the trunk. The big hospitality breakthrough for 1996 is sliding-glass technology for the side curtains. That, together with the less obstreperous road behavior, adds up to a better Viper, but no one will confuse it with a "nice" car. ●

The 1995 Viper, left, and the '96 makeover: Note new wheels, double-bubble hard top, and exhaust exiting at the snake's tail.

Variation on a Snake

Carroll Shelby, in collaboration with friend Dan Fitzgerald, is producing this Viper RT/10CS. It costs $22,660 more than a stock '96 Viper. The Shelby/Fitzgerald car features an open grille, a trunklid spoiler, blue "CS" emblems, and some autographs. Actually, a *lot* of autographs. Mr. Shelby's signature appears on both sides of the targa bar, on the glove-compartment door, on the steering wheel, and on a letter of authenticity tucked somewhere in the cockpit.

To be fair, there's some other stuff: Fitzgerald Motorsports installs free-flow exhausts, high-performance ignition wires, and a numerically higher final-drive ratio—3.73:1 versus the stock Viper's 3.07:1.

Only new Vipers purchased from Fitzgerald can be converted, although a few year-old models will be part of the mix (like the one shown here). In total, only 50 Vipers will be altered. The official CS introduction was in August, so about 49 are probably still left. Call 800-847-3715. —*Jo'Mar Heard*

DODGE VIPER RT/10

Vehicle type: front-engine, rear-wheel-drive, 2-passenger, 2-door roadster

Price as tested: $66,045

Price and option breakdown: base Dodge Viper RT/10 (includes $2675 luxury tax, $2600 gas-guzzler tax, and $700 freight), $61,975; hard top with sliding side curtains, $2500; air conditioning, $1200; luxury tax on options, $370

Major standard accessories: power steering, tilt steering

Sound system: Chrysler AM/FM-stereo radio/cassette, 6 speakers

ENGINE
Type ....V-10, aluminum block and heads
Bore x stroke ....4.00 x 3.88 in, 101.6 x 98.5mm
Displacement ....488 cu in, 7990cc
Compression ratio 9.1:1
Engine-control system.................Chrysler JTEC with port fuel injection
Emissions controls....................3-way catalytic converter, feedback fuel-air-ratio control
Valve gear........................pushrods, 2 valves per cylinder, hydraulic lifters
Power (SAE net)...............................415 bhp @ 5200 rpm
Torque (SAE net) ....488 lb-ft @ 3600 rpm
Redline ....6000 rpm

DRIVETRAIN
Transmission..6-speed
Final-drive ratio ....3.07:1, limited slip

Gear	Ratio	Mph/1000 rpm	Max. test speed
I	2.66	9.1	54 mph (6000 rpm)
II	1.78	13.6	81 mph (6000 rpm)
III	1.30	18.6	111 mph (6000 rpm)
IV	1.00	24.1	145 mph (6000 rpm)
V	0.74	32.6	173 mph (5300 rpm)
VI	0.50	48.3	140 mph (2900 rpm)

DIMENSIONS AND CAPACITIES
Wheelbase..96.2 in
Track, F/R..59.6/60.6 in
Length ....175.1 in
Width..75.7 in
Height...44.0 in
Ground clearance..5.0 in
Curb weight..3484 lb
Weight distribution, F/R....................................48.4/51.6%
Fuel capacity...19.0 gal
Oil capacity..11.0 qt
Water capacity..18.3 qt

CHASSIS/BODY
Type ....steel-tubing frame integral with body
Body material ....resin transfer-molded plastic

INTERIOR
SAE volume, front seat..49 cu ft
luggage space.....................................5 cu ft
Front seats..bucket
Seat adjustments ....fore and aft, seatback angle, lumbar support
Restraint systems, front..........door-mounted 3-point belts
General comfort ....poor fair **good** excellent
Fore-and-aft support...................poor fair good **excellent**
Lateral support ....poor fair **good** excellent

SUSPENSION
F: ....ind, unequal-length control arms, coil springs, anti-roll bar
R: ....ind, unequal-length control arms with a toe-control link, coil springs, anti-roll bar

STEERING
Type..rack-and-pinion, power-assisted
Turns lock-to-lock..2.3
Turning circle curb-to-curb..................................40.5 ft

BRAKES
F: ....13.0 x 1.3-in vented disc
R: ....13.0 x 0.9-in vented disc
Power assist ....vacuum

WHEELS AND TIRES
Wheel size ....F: 10.0 x 17 in, R: 13.0 x 17 in
Wheel type ....forged aluminum
Tires.....Michelin Pilot SX; F: 275/40ZR-17, R: 335/35ZR-17
Test inflation pressures, F/R ....29/29 psi

CAR AND DRIVER TEST RESULTS

ACCELERATION — Seconds
Zero to 30 mph...1.8
40 mph...2.4
50 mph...3.2
60 mph...4.1
70 mph...5.1
80 mph...6.5
90 mph...8.1
100 mph...9.8
110 mph...11.9
120 mph...14.2
130 mph...16.9
140 mph...20.3
150 mph...29.0
Street start, 5–60 mph......................................4.6
Top-gear passing time, 30–50 mph.................9.3
50–70 mph...9.1
Standing ¼-mile ....12.6 sec @ 113 mph
Top speed (drag limited).................................173 mph

BRAKING
70–0 mph @ impending lockup..................163 ft
Modulation..........................poor fair good **excellent**
Fade ....**none** light moderate heavy
Front-rear balance........................poor fair **good**

HANDLING
Roadholding, 300-ft-dia skidpad.................0.97 g
Understeer....................minimal **moderate** excessive

FUEL ECONOMY
EPA city driving...13 mpg
EPA highway driving......................................21 mpg
C/D observed fuel economy........................13 mpg

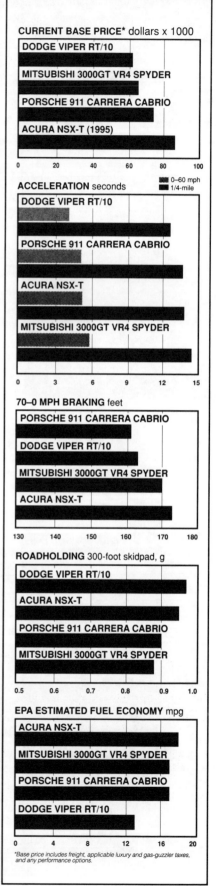

FIRST DRIVE

Dodge Viper GTS
The coupe cometh...at last

BY JOHN LAMM

FORGET ANY NOTION that the Dodge Viper GTS coupe is just a hardtop, fastback version of the RT/10 roadster. Open Vipers are wonderful playthings, a real hoot for a quick drive on a day neither too hot nor too wet on a road neither too bumpy nor too well patrolled. Weekend cars to blow out the week's worries. Viper coupes, however, are complete automobiles.

We sampled...that is, our Detroit Editor Ken Zino drove a prototype GTS coupe in 1995 (November issue), praising its power, damning its noise, and wondering which one—coupe or roadster—would dominate the sales race.

Now Dodge feels so strongly about the GTS's potential that it will build only Viper coupes—about 1700—during 1996. Next January the roadster (with many of the coupe's updates) will be folded back into the assembly mix, but Dodge figures the GTS will take 75–80 percent of future Viper sales.

How is the GTS different? Not the chassis, which is carried over with a general softening. The RT/10's front springs are used, but the rears are softer as are all the shocks. The coupe's tubular rear anti-roll bar is the same diameter as the RT/10's, but of 3.3-mm wall thickness versus 5.0.

And not the 8.0-liter V-10 engine, though it has been pumped up by further development to 450 bhp at 5200 rpm and 488 lb.-ft. of torque at 3700, and trimmed of 85 lb. thanks to lighter components.

But what a difference the body makes. Inheriting no body panels from the open Viper, the GTS is almost identical to the coupe show car, with outside electronic buttons you push to pop the door open. Inside, the seats are reshaped and lighter, and there are airbags for driver and passenger. Some of the analog instruments have been moved a bit, but the biggest changes are electrically operated glass windows and adjustable-height pedals.

The V-10 rumbles awake with that odd exhaust note. Cruising on the highway with the gearbox in 6th, the rpm are under 1500 and the exhaust is like mellow background music, entertaining without intruding into conversation.

The ride is reasonably smooth for a high-performance GT, firm but with none of the RT/10's jarring movements. Chrysler claims 60 mph comes up in 4.5 seconds. With a 0.39 C_D versus the RT/10's 0.50—and being 75 lb. lighter—the GTS can achieve a top speed of 185 mph, 20 above the open car's, according to Chrysler.

On a tight handling course, the GTS is a sweetheart. Although it understeers a bit more than the roadster, back off the gas, and the GTS will return to a neutral attitude. You can easily steer with the throttle, a little poke moving the back out, a big stab producing oversteer... all simply controlled.

And all this for $73,030, luxury and gas-guzzler taxes included. Not cheap, but a fair price for a car that has the promise of becoming one of the world's best Grand Touring machines.

■ **The GTS's fastback roof covers a new interior with dual airbags.**

PHOTOS BY THE AUTHOR

THE SPECIALTY FILE

Dodge Viper GTS-R

Can a professional wrestler compete in the Olympics?

BY DON SCHROEDER

PHOTOGRAPHY BY JEFFREY G. RUSSELL

It's mid-December at Atlanta Motor Speedway, sunny but 45 degrees, and the wind is blowing briskly across the infield of the big NASCAR oval. The temperature and low humidity suggest that the big V-10 engine in the Viper coupe droning around the infield track should have no problem cranking out its rated 650 horsepower, but it isn't.

Even though air is being rammed into this Viper's NACA hood intake at speeds above 160 mph, the V-10 is gasping for air. Engineers have discovered an unacceptable pressure drop across the race-prepared engine's stock air filters. "The dyno won't tell you this stuff, which is why we're here," says Viper engine chief Jerry Mallicoat.

That "we" also includes Viper engineer Gene Martindale, test drivers Neil Hannemann (the 1994 SCCA World Challenge champion) and Tommy Archer (of Archer Brothers fame on the Trans-Am circuit), and about two dozen other technicians, engineers, and supplier and team representatives. The

object of their attention is the Viper GTS-R, a pure racing version of the Viper GTS coupe that will run in three upcoming endurance races: the Rolex 24 Hours at Daytona in February, the Exxon Superflow 12 Hours of Sebring in March, and the Le Mans 24-hour race in France this June.

The last time Chrysler built a serious race car was in 1970, for the Trans-Am series. Of five factory-prepared entries, the Dodge Challenger and Plymouth Barracuda took the last two positions in points. Factory racing has become much more sophisticated since then. And now Chrysler wants to road-race its Viper. But wait. A big, burly, steel-framed V-10 Viper battling the likes of the lithe McLaren F1 exoticar, which was purpose-built for track racing? Or battling the Porsche 911 GT2, with more than 30 years of factory-backed track experience? Are these guys missing a few lug nuts?

Well, yes, sort of. The idea of a Viper as a race car is every bit as bold as the idea, six years ago, of a street Viper, approved for production when Chrysler didn't have any money and couldn't even build a competitive sedan. Like the street car, the GTS-R is being developed on a shoestring budget—just a few million dollars—and in fast-forward time. There will be

VIPER GTS-R

Engineer Gene Martindale consults with driver Tommy Archer between laps, above. The '96 Viper's new aluminum front and rear suspension is retained, but with metallic bushings. A Tilton master cylinder controls Brembo brake calipers, which squeeze giant 15-inch front and 13-inch rear discs.

barely a year from GTS-R's approval to its first trial-by-fire at the grueling Daytona 24-hour in February. The changes required of the Viper to make a GTS-R are extensive. By the time we looked at the car in mid-December—merely six weeks before its first race—nearly all of the modifications had been carved in stone.

The rules that this GTS-R will initially live under—FIA's, IMSA's, and ACO's GT class—require the GTS-R to retain its original frame. Welded onto that frame is a stress-relieved, 4130 chrome-moly alloy steel spaceframe, which increases the torsional stiffness of the frame to more than 18,500 pound-feet per degree, more than double that of the upcoming production Viper coupe frame.

The engine and transmission are lowered 2.5 inches and set back 2.8 inches in the frame for a lower center of gravity and improved weight distribution for racing—about 47/53 percent front/rear on the GTS-R versus 49/51 percent for the upcoming GTS coupe. Relocating the engine also allows frame cross-bracing over and in front of the engine, and it gives more clearance for the oil tank in the V-10's new dry-sump oil system.

For the engine, that's just the start. The racing V-10s, assembled by Caldwell Development, will be available in three forms. The standard "club" V-10 doesn't need many changes to make its 525 horsepower: just a racing camshaft with more lift and duration, and Borla headers. The "endurance" engine includes those changes, plus there's a velocity-stack intake manifold with ported heads, solid-lifter roller rockers, higher-rate valve springs, and chrome-moly Carillo connecting rods. Output is 650 horsepower. The "sprint" engine, at 700 horsepower, is an endurance engine with larger valves, an even more aggressive camshaft, and valvetrain changes that allow a higher 7000-plus-rpm redline. All three engines are based on the '97 block design, which was lightened and strengthened with new cast-in cylinder liners. Each optional engine will add about $30,000 to the GTS-R's expected $200,000 base price.

To boldly go where no Viper has gone before, Chrysler welcomed many original-equipment suppliers to its in-house effort. The transmission, for example, is a racing version of the Viper's Borg-Warner T-56 six-speed. The rear differential is a big Dana 60 with an aluminum case, specifically designed for the Viper GTS-R's tremendous torque (more than 650 pound-feet on the optional engines). The shock absorbers resemble Indy-car Konis, the steering rack is the Viper's stock TRW with revised valving, and the brakes from Brembo are whoppers—eight titanium pistons per caliper at the front, four-piston calipers at the rear, grasping either carbon-fiber or cast-iron discs. Michelin stepped in with custom Pilot SX racing slicks.

There's also a Tilton carbon-fiber triple-disc clutch and eight-pound flywheel (versus 32 pounds for the stock Viper). The center-lock three-piece BBS wheels have cast-magnesium centers. Goodyear racing tires will also be tested and offered.

All of this is wrapped up not by the Viper coupe's 350-pound resin-transfer-molded body, but one done completely in carbon fiber by Indy-car chassis builder Reynard, for a 200-pound weight savings. The body sports a biplane-type rear spoiler that increases downforce, although that will be changed to a single spoiler due to the sanctioning-body rule changes.

Nice résumé. But does it work? Chrysler wouldn't allow us behind the wheel to answer that question because the GTS-R being tested was the only one in existence. With the program timing already behind schedule, trashing the mule would mean . . . no program.

But we're sure that it has no problem going, stopping, and turning. At Sebring, Chrysler did some preliminary tests with our equipment and one of their drivers. With a stock transmission, an early endurance engine, and a lousy launch, the GTS-R still leapt to 60 mph in only 3.8 seconds. It continued accelerating as if a Saturn V booster were strapped to the roof: 100 mph in 7.1 seconds, the quarter-mile in 11.5 seconds at 132 mph. Top speed should be over 200 mph, a velocity the car could reach at Daytona or Le Mans.

VIPER GTS-R

Despite not being optimized for such a dainty task, the brakes can haul the 2910-pound Viper from 70 to 0 mph in 148 feet. Around one 140-foot-radius curve, the GTS-R was managing 1.90 g of grip, with negligible downforce from the rear wing.

As for its ability to get around the track, that's another story. The team has been track-testing frantically for a number of months, undeterred by weather, part failures, or even hawks crashing through the windshield at 140 mph (at Road Atlanta). At Sebring in early December, the car was understeering excessively at speed, the rear end was bouncing too much, the shock valving was all wrong, and the car was too hot inside. We asked 1995 Le Mans winner Andy Wallace, sitting in the cockpit after testing, if the GTS-R was fun to drive, and there was a pregnant pause, the result perhaps of years of talking to automotive writers. "It will be," he replied. Another pause. "When it's right, it will be fantastic fun," he added. Even the ever-smiling Martindale, putting in six 12-hour days a week as engineering chief since the GTS-R was approved, seemed weary.

And there was already good news. Driver Hannemann says the GTS-R's handling is quite forgiving—a relief from a car so closely related to such a brute-force street car. Just a few weeks later at Atlanta, the GTS-R had improved considerably. The problems at Sebring had mostly been solved, and the emphasis was now shifting toward driveline durability. "On a scale of one to ten, at Sebring, I'd say we were at four. Here at Atlanta, I'd call it a six or seven," said Martindale.

Engine guru Mallicoat was more smiles, too. The engine labs were reporting little wear from a recent teardown of the development engine. Furthermore, the motor was running well with relatively lean air-fuel ratios, meaning the GTS-R's Achilles' heel—uncompetitive fuel economy—was being improved. More promising were the lap times at Atlanta of under 1:19, exceeding the goals set by the team for the first time.

Chrysler intends the first four GTS-Rs (built at the company's new Conner Avenue assembly line in Detroit) to go directly to two racing teams: Canaska-Southwind Motorsports in Toronto, for the Daytona and Sebring events, and ORECA S.A. of France, for Le Mans. Assuming those races go as planned, the company will then offer between 30 and 50 GTS-Rs at an expected base price of $200,000, roughly the same as the Porsche but a steal compared with the nearly $1.1-million racing McLaren F1 car. Chrysler plans to sell most of the cars to racing teams. Second priority will be car collectors who want a piece of history. Good history, the company hopes. For the GTS-R to even finish at Daytona would be an accomplishment.

Critics have already tarred Chrysler's efforts with its still-young sports car as quixotic, but that's a bit like slagging the fat guy at the gym. The GTS-R is a remarkable display of corporate determination. Even if it fails to make it out of the pits, the engineers have already learned some lessons as a result of this program that they will apply to the 1997 Viper. The stock '97 heads will be derived from the GTS-R's, for example, and the block design has already been strengthened by what the team has learned.

One thing's for sure: Many eyes will be on this Viper in the next few months, and for once it won't be because of that hot curvy body. •

Development engine lurking beneath crossbraces is checked by motorhead Jerry Mallicoat.

Vehicle type: front-engine, rear-wheel-drive, 1-passenger, 2-door race car
Price as tested: $230,000 (estimated)
Engine type: pushrod 20-valve V-10, aluminum block and heads, Chrysler JTEC engine-control system with port fuel injection

Displacement	488 cu in, 7990cc
Power (SAE net)	650 bhp @ 6000 rpm
Torque (SAE net)	650 lb-ft @ 5000 rpm
Transmission	6-speed
Wheelbase	96.2 in
Length	176.0 in
Curb weight	2910 lb
Zero to 60 mph	3.8 sec
Zero to 100 mph	7.1 sec
Zero to 130 mph	11.2 sec
Standing ¼-mile	11.5 sec @ 132 mph
Top speed (estimated)	210 mph
Braking, 70–0 mph	148 ft
Roadholding, 140-ft-radius curve	1.90 g
Anticipated racing fuel economy	4 mpg

REALITY CHECK

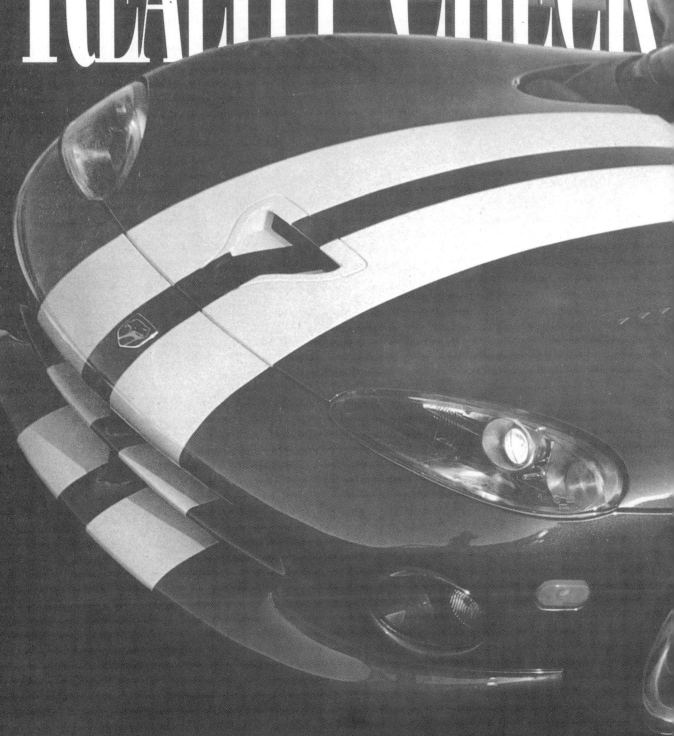

Is the Dodge Viper GTS coupe for real? We bring a Ferrari F355tb, a Porsche 911 Turbo, and a Chevrolet Corvette Grand Sport to the desert to find out.

BY JEAN LINDAMOOD

Phoenix—
We had to call twelve hotels to get rooms in downtown Phoenix for the Wednesday night before the Super Bowl, and when we checked in, we had to sign papers promising to check out in the morning. Then they saw the cars we were driving—a perfect red Ferrari F355tb; a sleek silver Porsche 911 Turbo; and an all-American red, white, and blue Chevrolet Corvette Grand Sport. Had we the time and the inclination, we could have stayed at the desk clerk's house that weekend. And he'd have bought the beer. ("I love you, man." "No, you can't drive the cars.")

No time for tailgating. We were on our way northwest to Wickenburg, Arizona, to meet up with the 1996 Indianapolis 500 pace car—the Dodge Viper GTS

PHOTOGRAPHY BY GREG JAREM

Hang on! The 450-bhp Dodge Viper GTS is loose in our land. It's more than a reskinned Viper RT/10, it's an all-new car. The interior is fresh and inviting; the steering wheel feels great in your mitts. It's eye-grabbing from every angle, and not a detail was missed—polished gas-cap cover is a nice touch.

Sometimes you just know when you're in the presence of goodness. And when 300 pound-feet of torque is belting you in the back, you're thinking nothing *but* goodness. Goodness *gracious*.

coupe. Think of ours as a scouting mission to see if the Viper GTS coupe had the consequence to make it in the big leagues. Is it real, or is it a cartoon car like the RT/10 roadster it closely follows? Make no mistake; the roadster is a blast and a half to tool around in, but there is a certain fragility of image about it. It's a rough-and-tumble show car with a license plate. Dodge doesn't make enough of them to care how anyone but its customers think about it, and that's okay. But now they are building a coupe, and it looks like the Viper has legs. If this is going to be an ongoing proposition, we need to know if Dodge is serious about building us the new American supercar.

We brought three of the world's most enduring (and endearing) supercars along as a reality check for the coupe. Not to see which was best, but to remind us of the unique qualities in each and to see if the Viper coupe belonged in the same company. It would be more of a meeting of the minds than a mingling of sheetmetal. The Dodge Boys had a pre-production Viper GTS coupe sequestered inside their proving ground compound and were scheduling drives around a cone course set up on their black asphalt lake. The Viper coupe could not come out to play, so I went in.

Helluva playmate, despite the fact that all we did was loop around some big flat track with a surface so smooth, you could've rolled a marble a mile. Sometimes you just know when you're in the presence of goodness. And when 300 pound-feet of torque is belting you in the back at about 1200 rpm, on its way to an eventual 480 pound-feet at 3600 rpm, you're thinking nothing *but* goodness. Goodness *gracious*.

Certainly the closest in paint job, if not in spirit, to the Viper GTS coupe is the Chevrolet Corvette Grand Sport. It seems to be the year for Pete Brock Daytona coupe paint jobs, so we have a metallic blue Vette striped in white (with two red hash marks on the left front quarter-panel) to go with our blue-with-white-stripes Viper coupe.

DODGE VIPER GTS
Front-engine, rear-wheel-drive coupe
2-passenger, 2-door composite body
Base price $66,000/price as tested $66,700
 (+ $2600 gas guzzler tax and luxury tax of 10%
 over $34,000)

ENGINE:
OHV V-10, aluminum block and heads
Bore x stroke 4.00 x 3.88 in (101.6 x 98.5 mm)
Displacement 488 cu in (7990 cc)
Compression ratio 9.6:1
Fuel system sequential multipoint injection
Power SAE net 450 bhp @ 5200 rpm
Torque SAE net 480 lb-ft @ 3600 rpm
Redline 6000 rpm

DRIVETRAIN:
6-speed manual transmission
Gear ratios (I) 2.66 (II) 1.78 (III) 1.30 (IV) 1.00
 (V) 0.74 (VI) 0.50
Final-drive ratio 3.07:1

MEASUREMENTS:
Wheelbase 96.2 in
Track front/rear 59.6/60.6 in
Length x width x height 176.7 x 75.7 x 47.0 in
Curb weight 3375 lb
Weight distribution front/rear 48/52%
Coefficient of drag 0.39
Fuel capacity 19.0 gal

SUSPENSION:
Independent front, with upper and lower A-arms,
 coil springs, dampers, anti-roll bar
Independent rear, with upper and lower A-arms,
 coil springs, dampers, anti-roll bar

STEERING:
Rack-and-pinion, power-assisted
Turns lock to lock 2.4
Turning circle 40.5 ft

BRAKES:
Vented discs front and rear

WHEELS AND TIRES:
17 x 10.0-in front, 17 x 13.0-in rear
 aluminum wheels
275/40ZR-17 front, 335/35ZR-17 rear
 Michelin Pilot SX tires

PERFORMANCE (manufacturer's data):
0–60 mph (estimated) in 4.5 sec
Standing 1/4-mile in 12.8 sec @ 109 mph
Top speed (estimated) 185 mph
EPA city driving 12 mpg

DIFFERENT MEANS, SAME END

Low tech versus high tech. Liters and horsepower against overhead cams and high revs. Flash against cash (lots of it). America against Europe, as it always has been and always will be.

Except, of course, that the comparison is misleading. The Corvette and the Viper have suspensions and braking systems similar to those of their European counterparts and ply their cornering power through even broader tire treads.

Both American cars use the same basic layout, of front engines driving the rear wheels. Where the Viper has composite panels on a tubular space frame, the Corvette uses fiberglass on a built-up steel structure. The Viper has an all-around dual A-arm suspension, while the Corvette has A-arms at the front and a lower A-arm and transverse-leaf setup at the back.

Neither engine is particularly avant-garde, both the Viper's 8.0-liter V-10 and the Corvette's 5.7-liter V-8 using pushrods to actuate their two valves per cylinder. Both engines are, however, high on horsepower and torque, the Viper leading with 450 bhp and 480 pound-feet, the Corvette having a more than adequate 330 bhp and 340 pound-feet. Both have six-speed manual transmissions, just like their European counterparts.

The European cars have engines behind the driver: The Ferrari's is sited amidships, and Porsche retains an engine behind the centerline of the rear wheels. Where the Porsche is a true unibody, the Ferrari has a central monocoque constructed of tubes and sheet steel. The Ferrari has double A-arms at all four corners and a clever adaptive damping system, while the Porsche has damper struts at the front and a quasi-A-arm arrangement at the back.

The Porsche is undoubtedly the more complex of the two: It has four-wheel drive, twin turbochargers for its horizontally opposed six-cylinder single-overhead-cam-per-bank 3.6-liter engine, and sophisticated traction control. Its 400 bhp

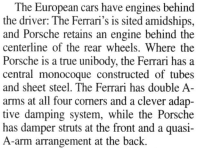

and 400 pound-feet come close to matching the Viper's power and torque output.

In order to inject more panache into its long-lived V-8 engine, Ferrari totally redesigned it, the twin overhead cams per bank now acting on three intake and two exhaust valves per cylinder. Yes, that's five valves per pot, making 40 in all. Although the numbers—375

bhp and 268 pound-feet—can't match those of the Porsche, this is the fastest-spinning engine here, producing peak power at 8250 rpm.

—Mark Gillies

No, really. Once you get past the initial shock of the retina-burning interior, the Corvette Grand Sport is still the two-seat rocket we have always loved. With big brakes and 330 bhp on tap, the old Vette remains an enthusiast's best friend. Power-on oversteer, anyone?

CHEVROLET CORVETTE GRAND SPORT
Front-engine, rear-wheel-drive coupe
2-passenger, 2-door composite body
Base price $37,225/price as tested $44,524
 (+ luxury tax of 10% over $34,000)

ENGINE:
OHV V-8, iron block, aluminum heads
Bore x stroke 4.00 x 3.48 in (101.6 x 88.4 mm)
Displacement 350 cu in (5735 cc)
Compression ratio 10.8:1
Fuel system sequential multipoint injection
Power SAE net 330 bhp @ 5800 rpm
Torque SAE net 340 lb-ft @ 4500 rpm
Redline 6300 rpm

DRIVETRAIN:
6-speed manual transmission
Gear ratios (I) 2.64 (II) 1.78 (III) 1.30 (IV) 1.00
 (V) 0.74 (VI) 0.49
Final-drive ratio 3.45:1

MEASUREMENTS:
Wheelbase 96.2 in
Track front/rear 57.7/59.1 in
Length x width x height 178.5 x 70.7 x 46.3 in
Curb weight 3298 lb
Weight distribution front/rear 52/48%
Fuel capacity 20.0 gal

SUSPENSION:
Independent front, with upper and lower control
 arms, coil springs, dampers, anti-roll bar
Independent rear, with lower control arms,
 transverse monoleaf spring, dampers, anti-roll bar

STEERING:
Rack-and-pinion, power-assisted
Turns lock to lock 2.25
Turning circle 40.0 ft

BRAKES:
Vented discs front and rear
Anti-lock system

WHEELS AND TIRES:
17 x 9.5-in front, 17 x 11.0-in rear
 aluminum wheels
275/40ZR-17 front, 315/35ZR-17 rear
 Goodyear Eagle GS-C tires

PERFORMANCE:
0-60 mph (estimated) in 5.2 sec
Top speed (estimated) 155 mph
EPA city driving 17 mpg

It's the only color scheme for each, with the Viper's being the more tasteful of the two by virtue of the Corvette's lipstick-red leather interior. Wargh! Uff! Uff!

Zany decoration aside, the Corvette is possibly the best-looking, best-engineered car in America. It's not as special to drive as it once was, but the Corvette is still astonishingly easy to flail in the extreme, if somewhat brutal and harsh on rough pavement. Even the youngster among us, Mark Schirmer, admitted that it was hard to believe the Corvette, with 330 horsepower on tap, was "the weak sister in this slugfest. It doesn't feel underpowered—I think the others are just overpowered. Not a bad thing," he hastens to add.

If you are looking for a dollar-for-dollar thrill, you win the jackpot with Chevy's $44,000 slot car. For now, that is. It seems quite likely that the Viper coupe has what it takes to steal the Corvette's thunder as America's supercar when it starts rolling off the Viper line this month. (No Viper roadsters will be built from April to December of this year while 1700 GTS coupes are coming together. This is not a car you will see coming and going.)

Exclusive it may be, but the Viper GTS coupe will still sell for a very reasonable base price of $66,000 (before luxury and gas taxes are slapped on). Added to that, the GTS coupe is "stonking" fast, as our very British executive editor Mark Gillies puts it, almost shooting out from underneath you when you put yourself into it right-foot-first. Unofficial 0-to-60-mph acceleration times from the 450-bhp, 8.0-liter V-10 have been in the low-four-second range, with quarter-miles coming in under thirteen seconds.

Performance times are almost immaterial once you hear the thunder generated by the effort. Yes, it sounds good now, with the exhaust system tucked under the car and feeding to the rear where it belongs. Dodge has embraced the notion that good sound is a good thing to have in your supercar.

Not that the Viper coupe sounds as good as a Ferrari F355tb. But then, a Ferrari is pure sound and beauty and fury. It is sensuous, not sensible. A car you want to drive fast in the lowest gear possible just to hear that engine howl. The Ferrari's relatively small 375-bhp, 3.5-liter V-8 (with five valves per cylinder) looks small and neat and very serious nestled in the engine compartment. It is all Ferrari and most special.

The Dodge Viper GTS coupe was parked next to a Ferrari 456GT inside the Chrysler test track.

"We didn't benchmark the Ferrari, I want you to know this," said Herb Helbig, the fourth guy assigned to Team Viper seven years ago and the guy in charge of vehicle synthesis. "It's here because it represents the passion people have for automobiles. Cars that have some magic quality that has the hair standing up on the backs of your arms when you turn the key and hear the engine come to life.

"There aren't too many people at Ferrari who don't understand cars," said Helbig, running his hand over the oil-filler cap. The Viper coupe has a polished metal industrial-looking gas cap. Unfortunately, it's just a cover over the government-regulation screw-type plastic filler cap. Oh, well. But there are some thoughtful touches on the Viper that say someone here did understand what he was doing.

One deserving of special mention is the

FERRARI F355 BERLINETTA
Mid-engine, rear-wheel-drive coupe
2-passenger, 2-door aluminum and steel body
Base price $115,600/price as tested $115,600
 (+ $5400 gas guzzler tax and luxury tax of 10% over $34,000)

ENGINE:
40-valve DOHC V-8, aluminum block and heads
Bore x stroke 3.35 x 3.03 in (85.1 x 77.0 mm)
Displacement 213 cu in (3495 cc)
Compression ratio 11.0:1
Fuel system sequential multipoint injection
Power SAE net 375 bhp @ 8250 rpm
Torque SAE net 268 lb-ft @ 6000 rpm
Redline 8500 rpm

DRIVETRAIN:
6-speed manual transmission
Gear ratios (I) 3.74 (II) 2.63 (III) 1.96 (IV) 1.55 (V) 1.26 (VI) 1.02
Final-drive ratio 3.56:1

MEASUREMENTS:
Wheelbase 96.5 in
Track front/rear 59.6/63.6 in
Length x width x height 167.3 x 74.8 x 46.1 in
Curb weight 2976 lb
Weight distribution front/rear 43/57%
Fuel capacity 21.7 gal

SUSPENSION:
Independent front, with upper and lower A-arms, coil springs, dampers, anti-roll bar
Independent rear, with upper and lower A-arms, coil springs, dampers, anti-roll bar

STEERING:
Rack-and-pinion, variable-power-assisted
Turns lock to lock 3.2
Turning circle 37.9 ft

BRAKES:
Vented discs front and rear
Anti-lock system

WHEELS AND TIRES:
18 x 7.5-in front, 18 x 10.0-in rear aluminum wheels
225/40ZR-18 front, 265/40ZR-18 rear Bridgestone Expedia S-01 tires

PERFORMANCE (manufacturer's data):
0–60 mph in 4.6 sec
Standing 1/4-mile in 13.0 sec @ 112 mph
Top speed 183 mph
EPA city driving 17 mpg

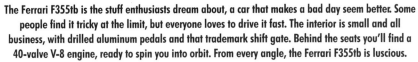
The Ferrari F355tb is the stuff enthusiasts dream about, a car that makes a bad day seem better. Some people find it tricky at the limit, but everyone loves to drive it fast. The interior is small and all business, with drilled aluminum pedals and that trademark shift gate. Behind the seats you'll find a 40-valve V-8 engine, ready to spin you into orbit. From every angle, the Ferrari F355tb is luscious.

Porsche 911 Turbo: 400 bhp, 400 pound-feet of torque, a six-speed gearbox, four-wheel drive—this is the high-speed tool we all want parked in our garage. It is easy to drive fast, and *fast* is how you drive it. The cabin is upright and proper; the seats are firm and comfortable. And the brakes? They may be the best in the business.

> All I know is that I want to drive the Porsche Turbo fast just to feel it go. At 80 mph, you can toe the accelerator and the turbo blows an instant burst of speed at you.

adjustable pedal set. In a display of stunning creative thinking and engineering, the Viper team realized that being able to adjust the pedal height was much more crucial to a proper driving position than being able to adjust the seat track. A mechanical cable-worm-gear system operated by a twist knob under the dash raises and lowers all three pedals—accelerator, brake, and clutch—in unison, as your arms remain the correct distance from the steering wheel. Cool.

Most impressive, the coupe weighs an unbelievable seventy pounds less than the roadster, thanks to extensive computer work. Something like fifteen pounds were saved in each corner of the suspension. At the same time, the coupe's structure is 25

PORSCHE 911 TURBO
Rear-engine, 4-wheel-drive coupe
2+2-passenger, 2-door steel body
Base price $105,000/price as tested $107,770
(+ $2600 gas guzzler tax and luxury tax of 10% over $34,000)

ENGINE:
Twin-turbocharged and intercooled SOHC horizontally opposed 6, aluminum block and heads
Bore x stroke 3.94 x 3.01 in (100.0 x 76.4 mm)
Displacement 220 cu in (3605 cc)
Compression ratio 8.0:1
Fuel system sequential multipoint injection
Turbochargers KKK
Maximum boost pressure 11.6 psi
Power SAE net 400 bhp @ 5750 rpm
Torque SAE net 400 lb-ft @ 4500 rpm
Redline 6720 rpm

DRIVETRAIN:
6-speed manual transmission
Gear ratios (I) 3.82 (II) 2.15 (III) 1.56 (IV) 1.21 (V) 0.97 (VI) 0.75
Final-drive ratio 3.44:1

MEASUREMENTS:
Wheelbase 89.4 in
Track front/rear 55.6/59.3 in
Length x width x height 167.7 x 70.7 x 51.8 in
Curb weight 3307 lb
Weight distribution front/rear 40/60%
Coefficient of drag 0.34
Fuel capacity 19.4 gal

SUSPENSION:
Independent front, with damper struts, lower control arms, coil springs, anti-roll bar
Independent rear, with upper and lower A-arms, dampers, coil springs, anti-roll bar

STEERING:
Rack-and-pinion, variable-power-assisted
Turns lock to lock 2.47
Turning circle 38.5 ft

BRAKES:
Vented discs front and rear
Anti-lock system

WHEELS AND TIRES:
18 x 8.0-in front, 18 x 10.0-in rear aluminum wheels
225/40ZR-18 front, 285/30ZR-18 rear Bridgestone Potenza S-02 tires

PERFORMANCE (manufacturer's data):
0–60 mph in 4.4 sec
Standing 1/4-mile in 12.7 sec
Top speed 180 mph
EPA city driving 13 mpg

percent stiffer, and you can really feel it on the track.

Back to the question of beauty. There are those who believe the F355tb is one of the best Ferraris yet. It is certainly the most sensuous and elegant among our esteemed group. So do the Viper's looks shape up? Well, you would not call it elegant, but striking, yes.

Although the original GTS coupe show car was built using an old Indy pace car Viper roadster as its base, the production Viper coupe shares only the exterior door panels and a handful of insignificant pieces like the side mirrors, a hinge cover, and a few trim parts. "The ashtray is probably the only K-car part left in the corporation," says executive Viper engineer Roy Sjoberg. Every change made from roadster to coupe made this Viper more real until it became a wonderful new, all-of-a-piece automobile with a very touchable personality.

Fenders bulge sensuously in your view from the cockpit, with the hood swelling between them. The roof sweeps into the body at just the right places, and the sills make an interesting diversion where exhaust pipes used to be. Functioning NACA ducts pull air in through the hood.

The Viper team also did a lovely job of bonding the all-glass backlight to the body. The hardware for lifting the backlight up (for access to the trunk) is also bonded to the glass for a clean look devoid of the usual beauty bolts needed to secure metal to glass.

No, it's not a Ferrari, but listen to Mark Schirmer: "The Viper coupe made me question my firm belief that the Ferrari dealership would be my first destination the morning after I become grotesquely rich." Sometimes you just know when you're in the presence of goodness.

Make that greatness when you take the wheel of a Porsche 911 Turbo. "The Porsche is utterly functional," says Michael Jordan. "As devoid of pretense as a force vector in a physics equation."

What the hell does that mean? All I know is that I want to drive the Porsche Turbo fast just to feel it go. At 80 mph, you can toe the accelerator and the turbo blows an instant burst of speed at you. Oh, my Lord in heaven. Whatever, whenever, wherever—this car will do it. You can barely contain yourself, foot hovering in space over the accelerator as the speedometer edges back down to eighty. And there you are again, doing 100 mph over the speed limit. The Porsche Turbo is monstrously exhilarating and ridiculously civilized at that speed. Somehow, um, sensible. I think it's the upright-citizen position you're in behind the wheel. That and the no-joke brakes.

Does the Viper coupe have anything approaching the perfection of the Porsche in its makeup? Perhaps in its comfortable cockpit, in the friendliness of its huge gobs of torque.

It's the sum total of its parts that makes the Viper GTS coupe the real deal—a serious car with genuine heritage. The price is reasonable, and the experience of owning one ought to be extraordinary. It can be counted with the stars. As Michael Jordan so eloquently puts it, "If you were to start a car company, these are the cars you would build. They demonstrate that the intuitive approach to automobile design is far superior to the focus-group approach. They are not meant to make sense. They do not comfort, coddle, or reassure. They do not take care, plan fastidiously, or camp only in designated areas. What are these cars about? You might as well wonder why hawks should fly.

"But to drive these cars is to be in a world where the colors are brighter, scents stronger, and sensations more powerful. The world feels full of drama, as if there were heroes abroad in the land, and at any moment you might meet Albert Einstein, Pablo Picasso, or at least Carroll Shelby."

Amen.

DODGE VIPER GTS

Undercover retro rocket

BY ANDREW BORNHOP
PHOTOS BY RON SESSIONS

Consider this: Every single Dodge Viper GTS coupe that rolls out of the Connor Avenue assembly plant in Detroit comes equipped with air conditioning, leather upholstery, power windows, power door locks, dual airbags, an anti-theft alarm and an in-dash CD player with six speakers.

Cushy, cushy, cushy.

Has our elemental friend the Viper gone soft?

Not for a moment. In spite of the amenities and weatherproof cockpit,

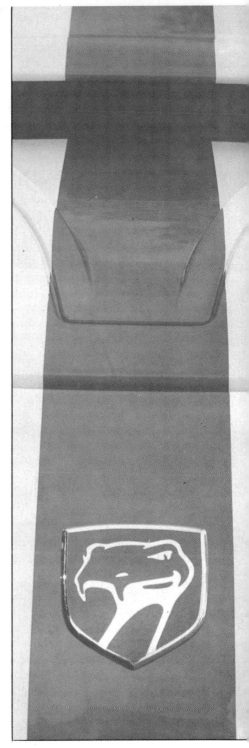

this GTS remains a menacing Viper at heart, one that's—dare I say it—more brutish, more raw, than the Viper RT/10 roadster.

Fire up the engine and you'll immediately see why. The 488-cu-in. aluminum V-10 settles into a burbly 700-rpm idle that's far lumpier than the RT/10's. A new camshaft? You bet, one with increased duration to help bump output from the roadster's already stout 415 bhp at 5200 rpm to a whopping 450 at the same rpm. And though the 490 lb-ft of torque (at 3700 rpm) represents only a small gain, it's nevertheless an improvement on the wheel-spinning mother lode of 488 at 3600 already on tap in the 1996 RT/10 roadster.

It's more than just its cam, however, that ups the GTS's power. The new heads have better flow, and coolant passages nearer to hot spots such as the sparkplugs and valve seats allow Chrysler to bump the compression from 9.1:1 to 9.6:1. The rear-exit exhaust is also new, less restrictive but still making the odd sound only twin banks of five cylinders can make. It's not a V-8 roar; it's a deep bellow that never sounds strained, not even at the 6000-rpm redline.

The GTS's 90-degree V-10 is also 80 lb lighter than the RT/10's, thanks primarily to lighter heads and a new thin-wall aluminum block with dry cast-iron cylinder liners. Moreover, the GTS engine now has reverse-flow cooling (like GM's LT1 V-8) that allows Chrysler to use a half-gallon less coolant than before. This lets the engine reach operating temperature more quickly to reduce cold-start emissions and saves the GTS a few pounds.

Other weight-reduction efforts include new seats that save 20 lb and a new, more rigid frame that cuts another 60. And beneath the GTS's seductive blue skin are new cast-aluminum control arms, hub carriers and steering knuckles (replacing ones made of stamped steel and cast iron), saving a hefty 15 lb of unsprung weight at each corner. By our scales, the GTS comes in at 3380 lb, 60 lb less than the RT/10 roadster. Impressive, considering that the new roof (with glass) adds 100 lb, and the dual airbags another 28.

With the reduced weight and additional power, you'd expect this GTS to be quicker than the roadster. It is. In fact, at 4.4 sec to 60 mph and the quarter mile in 12.8 sec at 116.2 mph, the GTS is the fastest production Viper we've tested.

Stopping, however, proves more difficult for the Viper coupe. Distances of 158 ft from 60 mph and 262 ft from 80 mph are good, but not what they could (or should) be. With vented 13.0-in. rotors and 4-piston calipers at each wheel, it's not a lack of stopping power. What the GTS needs is ABS, because the front wheels lock easily and brake pressure is difficult to modulate properly. ABS, Chrysler will remind us, is simply not in tune with the Viper's "keep-it-simple" spirit. Maybe so, but this GTS, unlike the roadster, can (and will) be used when the weather is wet.

The GTS weaves through our 700-ft slalom like a true Viper should, aided by a small but predictable amount of understeer on its way to a 63.5-mph run. A bit more understeer is present on our skidpad, where the Dodge circles at an impressive 0.97g. Steady throttle means steady understeer, but a quick lift of the pedal means you'll soon be looking out the side window with the GTS's tail hung out wide. And the torquey 10-cylinder—if you had any doubts—keeps the back end out under power ... with ease.

The Viper coupe's tendency to understeer a bit more than the roadster doesn't come as a surprise, given that its springs and rear anti-roll bar are softer. The GTS, however, does not feel floaty, partly because of new rear-suspension geometry that lowers the car's roll center and minimizes toe change during wheel travel. Softer shock absorbers are also used all around, a change felt in the GTS's ride, which is more supple than the

roadster's, especially on bumpy roads.

So is the new GTS Chrysler's version of a Corvette? No way. The GTS isn't nearly as refined. And it isn't meant to be. This is still very much a Viper: Its interior smells like glue when the engine is hot, you can hear gear rattle when the car is idling in neutral, and it's just about impossible to creep around in low gear without experiencing some driveline lash.

Why then, is it so seductive? Simply put, it's unique, and it has in spades what most car enthusiasts crave: lots of horsepower and torque, big tires and plenty of style.

Inspired by Peter Brock's Cobra Daytona Coupe, the GTS is a throwback to the Sixties, a twin-striped racing car for the street, a car blessed with more than a few luscious curves.

The body itself is made of a fiberglass reinforced plastic, sharing no parts at all with the roadster's. It's also much sleeker, with a drag coefficient of 0.35 versus the roadster's 0.50. The improved aerodynamics and increased power result in a top speed of 185 mph, about 15 mph better than the RT/10's.

Countless details adorn the GTS body, and a few are particularly noteworthy. The exterior door handles, for instance, are little L-shape pieces recessed into the black rear portion of each door. A simple push of a button (integrated into the handle) triggers a solenoid that electrically unlatches the door. Electric latches on a Viper? Out of place, yes, but needed to let the side windows fully retract into the GTS's shallow doors.

Other neat GTS bits are the NACA

The GTS is a throwback to the 60s, a twin-striped racing car for the street.

duct on the hood and the racing-style aluminum fuel-filler cap. The duct is functional, feeding air directly to the engine for a ram-air effect at speed. The cap, however, is purely esthetic. It looks great, just like it has been pulled right off a Cobra. But when you pop it open, you'll see that it hides a conventional twist-off gas cap.

No big deal; you forget about such incidentals when you drive the GTS. Getting into the car isn't easy, what with its low roof, wide doorsills and deep bucket seats. Once in, though, there's plenty of room for those long of leg, torso or both. And via a knob below the GTS's 3-spoke magnesium steering wheel, the pedal height can be tailored to each driver. Still, there isn't any place to put your left foot when it's not on the clutch.

The gauges are analog dials, easily read and mounted in a revised dash that blends neatly into the door panels.

A passenger airbag resides where you'd expect a glovebox, which is now found in the rearmost portion of the GTS's very wide center console. Unique to the GTS is a rotary headlight switch; this, because the old pull-on/push-off switch would occasionally get turned off by the driver's left knee. A lack of space has also played a role in Chrysler's choice of power windows—there simply isn't enough width in the cockpit for conventional cranks.

As exotics go, the Viper GTS is one hell of a bargain.

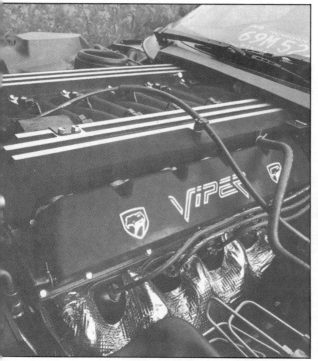

The GTS's bucket seats offer more lateral support than the roadster's and prove to be comfortable over the long haul, helped by an inflatable lumbar support. Curiously, the shoulder harness passes over your inboard shoulder, which tends to catch people off guard.

The GTS, however, seldom does. It's remarkably easy to drive. Dump the clutch from just above idle and you're on your way. The abundance of torque keeps the car from being the least bit finicky. It doesn't seem to matter what gear you're in, as long as you're moving. The gearshift lever feels robust (as it should, considering that it's mounted right above the 6-speed box) and the gates are well defined. Actuation of the clutch—which is a quarter-inch larger in diameter than in the roadster—is simple, and the pedal effort isn't as high as you might expect. The pedals are also properly positioned for heel-and-toe downshifting. If, however, the GTS is shifted out of 1st gear at low rpm, a device shunts the lever over to 4th gear.

This never happened with us because the GTS invites hard driving and absolutely relishes bursts up to triple-digit speeds in 3rd and 4th gears. The rack-and-pinion steering feels naturally weighted, though the ratio is quick enough to make the GTS feel almost darty. Complicating things is the car's tendency to follow seams in the pavement, likely attributable to the significant width of the 275/40ZR-17 front Michelin Pilots.

These tires have been designed for better wet-weather grip, which obviously isn't much of a concern with the roofless Viper. In our dry tests they provide excellent grip in turns, helping the GTS corner with good balance and composure. When the back end does break loose—as can happen when you unload the rears and immediately get back on the throttle—it does so more predictably than in the roadster.

On the road, engine and rolling noise both make their way into the GTS cabin, making the car louder inside than, say, a Corvette. But normal-volume conversation is now at least possible on the highway, something that's not true in the RT/10. Wind noise isn't a concern and the side windows are firmly anchored, never fluttering at high speed.

Simply put, there's nothing on the market just like a GTS, apart from, maybe, an RT/10 roadster. But remember, the GTS is weatherproof. And you can roll up its windows and lock it like a normal car.

The GTS, first and foremost, is a Viper. And that means it's a basic car, but one that just happens to have a better power-to-weight ratio than a Porsche 911 Turbo. One that, like a Harley-Davidson, could be built only in America. And, as exotics go, one that's a hell of a bargain. At $73,030 (there are no options), all 1750 GTS coupes being built in 1996 will be gobbled up fast.

Who would have ever thought the K-car company could build something this wild?

DODGE VIPER GTS

PRICE
List price, all POE	$66,000
Price as tested	$73,030

Price as tested includes std equip. (dual airbags, leather upholstery, height-adj pedals, AM/FM/CD/cassette stereo, central locking, tilt steering wheel, pwr windows & mirrors, anti-theft alarm), luxury tax ($3730), gas-guzzler tax ($2600), dest charge ($700).

ENGINE
Type	ohv V-10
Displacement	7990 cc
Bore x stroke	101.6 x 98.5 mm
Compression ratio	9.6:1
Horsepower, SAE net	450 bhp @ 5200 rpm
Torque	490 lb-ft @ 3700 rpm
Maximum engine speed	6000 rpm
Fuel injection	elect. sequential port
Fuel requirement	premium unleaded

GENERAL DATA
Curb weight	3380 lb
Weight distribution, f/r, %	49/51
Wheelbase	96.2 in.
Track, f/r	59.6/60.6 in.
Length	176.7 in.
Width	75.7 in.
Height	47.0 in.
Trunk space	6.1 cu ft

CHASSIS & BODY
Layout	front engine/rear drive
Body/frame	resin transfer molded composite/tubular steel
Brakes, f/r	13.0-in. vented discs/13.0-in. vented discs, vacuum assist
Wheels	cast-alloy, 17 x 10 f, 17 x 13 r
Tires	Michelin Pilot MXX3 275/40ZR-17 f, 335/35ZR-17 r
Steering	rack & pinion, power assist
Turns, lock to lock	2.4
Suspension, f/r	unequal-length A-arms, coil springs, tube shocks, anti-roll bar/unequal-length A-arms, toe links, coil springs, tube shocks, anti-roll bar

DRIVETRAIN
Transmission .... 6-sp manual

Gear	Ratio	Overall Ratio	(Rpm)	Mph
1st	2.66:1	8.17:1	(6000)	53
2nd	1.78:1	5.46:1	(6000)	80
3rd	1.30:1	3.99:1	(6000)	110
4th	1.00:1	3.07:1	(6000)	142
5th	0.74:1	2.27:1	est (5550)	185
6th	0.50:1	1.54:1	est (4010)	185

Final-drive ratio 3.07:1
Engine rpm @ 60 mph, top gear ...... 1300 rpm

ACCELERATION
Time to speed	Seconds
0-30 mph	2.0
0-40 mph	2.7
0-50 mph	3.7
0-60 mph	4.4
0-70 mph	5.5
0-80 mph	7.0
0-90 mph	8.3
0-100 mph	9.8

Time to distance
0-100 ft	3.0
0-500 ft	7.2
0-1320 ft (1/4 mile)	12.8 sec @ 116.2 mph

BRAKING
Minimum stopping distance
From 60 mph	158 ft
From 80 mph	262 ft
Control	good
Overall brake rating	good

HANDLING
Lateral accel (200-ft skidpad)	0.97g
Speed thru 700-ft slalom	63.5 mph

FUEL ECONOMY
Normal driving	est 14.0 mpg
Fuel economy (EPA city/hwy)	13/24 mpg
Fuel capacity	19.0 gal.

Subjective ratings consist of excellent, very good, good, average, poor
est estimated
na means information is not available

CHRYSLER VIPER GTS-R

Warming the snake's blood

Andrew Frankel straps himself into a Viper GTS-R, and experiences 700bhp of fierce GT racer

The noise is so loud it makes your inner ear itch. Everybody in the pits at Paul Ricard takes an involuntary step back as the Chrysler Viper GTS-R draws its first breath of the new day and settles down to an angry 2000rpm idle as the electronic management runs through its warm-up strategies.

The sound of the beast wrested from its slumbers, it should be said, is not nice. Not yet at least. But as a device to grab your attention and remind you of the potential crammed within those extraordinary lines, it is uniquely compelling. Liquid crystal numbers flicker and dance on the dash, a man with a lap-top plugs into the engine diagnostics to discover what kind of mood it's in today. Thumbs point north and then the 8-litre racing motor is shut down, leaving just a crashing, echoing silence racing through the pits. Someone opens the cockpit door and points. At me.

It would be easy to suggest that the Viper GTS-R is not a terribly good racing car. Throughout its first season in the BPR championship, it has never won a race. The best result for the French Oreca team which runs the cars was the sixth and eighth places achieved in its last race of the season at Nogaro. In a season dominated by just two marques, the likes of the Viper were left licking at scraps, knowing that the best possible result would be first across the line after the warring Porsches and McLarens.

What the statistics fail to show is that a Viper costs about one quarter of the price of a McLaren, even less when compared with the Porsche. But, as Neil Hannemann, the man who runs the racing Viper programme for Chrysler, is keen to point out: "They don't hand out prizes for the first car across the line costing less than a million dollars."

They should. In terms of results achieved for money spent, the Viper project is every bit as impressive as any other. Not least because the start point for the project, the road-going Viper GTS is a technological brontosaurus compared with one such as the McLaren. Where that has a mid-mounted, quad-cam, 48-valve V12 built by BMW exclusively for McLaren, the Viper has a pushrod 10-cylinder motor found not simply in the front of Vipers but also Chrysler pick-ups and trucks. Where Britain uses a Formula 1 style carbon fibre monocoque, the US uses a conventional steel spaceframe... Under the circumstances, it's a credit to the Viper that it even made it onto the same grid.

There is still a remarkable amount of road-car left in the Viper, supporting Chrysler's view that GT racing should be for race-fettled road cars, not the other way around, a point seemingly lost on Porsche. The Viper GTS-R uses the same block and heads as its road-going equivalent and the same gearbox too, albeit with strengthened internals and modified ratios.

Climb aboard and the Viper-literate will recognise the driving position and even the carbon fibre dash that's been moulded to silhouette that of the road car. Otherwise, though, it's pure race car and more than a little scary just to sit in, let alone drive.

It won't start until you've flicked on two petrol pumps, switched on the computers, hit the ignition, turned on the cooling for the diff, the fans for the rear brakes and thumbed the starter button. And then there's a very big bang.

Olivier Beretta leans in. He's the current team hotshot, a 27-year-old ex-F1 driver

Interior of the racing Viper remains surprisingly close to that of the road car. Other carried over parts include the steel spaceframe chassis and gearbox

Viper looks aggressive and purposeful on the move, and is a great sight howling around the track. Styling similar to road-going GTS, bar huge rear wing

who's driving quicker right now than Le Mans winner Eric Helary and team-mate Justin Bell, described as "an extremely good endurance driver". Beretta is having a ball right now. Oreca is based at Ricard, just a couple of hours from his home in Monaco. Unsurprisingly, he feels he still has unfinished business in Formula 1, his proudest result being an eighth place in his home grand prix in '94. Still, he's happy with the Viper and its official 650bhp, especially as it's really about 700bhp.

"Be careful with the brakes," comes his cheery suggestion. "They're carbon discs and until you warm them up, they do not work. At all. Not much grip from the tyres either." He grins and trots across to the other GTS-R, fitted with a passenger seat, to reacquaint some poor innocent with the instinct of survival. So now I have to watch my tyres, my brakes and my mirrors.

Mercifully, the GTS-R is not difficult to drive. You, every bit as well as me, could pull out of the pits without stalling, rumble round the track and return in one piece. You'd find appalling driveline shunt if you drove too slowly but if you went at, say, modern Ford Escort effort, it would prove easy and, thanks to the power steering, effortless to drive too.

The problem is, I just can't go at Ford Escort pace, not with perhaps only a dozen laps in the car and Monsieur Beretta out there, nibbling at his personal best.

It's hilarious when cold. If the non-existent brakes don't get you on the way into the corner, the tyres will finish the job at the exit. It occurred to me, as I took my

Titanic 8-litre V10 is carried from the road car

first ever look from inside a racing car at the everlasting straight at Ricard, that it would have looked slightly more professional if I'd approached it on slightly less than full opposite lock.

With sprint gearing and medium wing settings, the Viper's top speed is cut from a potential 210mph back to around 180mph. On the straight, that means all intermediate gears are consumed pretty much as the clutch comes up. Sixth actually lasts quite a long time, long enough for sure to play bored race hero at 170mph, drumming thumbs on the wheel and looking forward impatiently to the next corner.

Back in the real world, I wasn't looking forward to it at all. Beretta comes bellowing past and turns in flat in fifth at not much less than 150mph; for this is Signes, one of the toughest and fastest corners in racing.

Despite using ultra-powerful carbon fibre disc brakes, the 1250kg car still struggles to shed speed

I have no idea how fast I tackled it, perhaps in the mid 130s, and there, in an instant, the GTS-R felt like a racing car, not the ludicrously hotted-up road car I was suspecting it might be. Clamped down by the wings, I was able to guide the warmed Viper with a precision I hadn't imagined.

Around the rest of the lap it proved fabulously easy to drive fast. The engine's on song from 2500rpm and puts 650lb ft of torque through the rear slicks at not much more, while the handling is broadly neutral but happy to indulge in quick third gear slides whenever the mood takes you. What impresses most is that it's almost agile, a hitherto unheard of commodity in Viper circles. Only under braking does it feel every one of its 1250kg, even with the discs up to temperature. Beretta says that it can get tricky at qualifying pace. I'm afraid we'll just have to take his word for it.

Most importantly, the Viper GTS-R felt how I'd hoped a sports car would: a racer through and through but one closely related to the road car on which it is based.

Even so, what I perceive to be its greatest strength is actually its weakness. A car this honest is never going to keep up with a true racer such as the Porsche GT1. Which is why Chrysler is off to seek fame and fortune in the lesser GT2 category this season. It may not have the kudos, but it should take some class wins and possibly the championship.

If the Porsches race again, you can, as ever, expect to see them droning around in convoy way ahead of the field. If you're looking to be impressed, they'll do fine; if its excitement you want, take a look at the Vipers: being cheap, fun and full of heart may not win you races, but it will win you friends. That is exactly what Chrysler wants and, with the Viper GTS-R, that is exactly what it deserves.

Viper's evocative stripes are an American trademark, harking back to the days of the fearsome Cobra

Viper GTS-R vs McLaren F1 GTR

Mechanically, they are paper plane and space shuttle. But you knew that already. Sending Britain's carbon fibre wondercar, with its variably valve timed, quad-cam, 48-valve V12 BMW motor, out to fight Chrysler's steel chassised, truck-engined Viper might not seem exactly fair, but these, when I drove them, were not the differences I perceived most strongly.

When I drove the Viper, it was dry, the team relaxed, the track wide open and familiar; the car at the end of its tour of duty. When I drove the McLaren, 18-months earlier, it was damp, the team tense, the track more suited to hatchback racing and known to me only from a couple of laps

completed in a Vauxhall Nova six years previously. The car carried Britain's best chance of victory at Le Mans, which was just five weeks away, and Mark Blundell had just spun it on the puddles before bringing it in for my turn. It was on slicks.

Sadly, I discovered rather more about myself than the McLaren that day, though I'll remember its noise and crushing acceleration long after I've forgotten that feeling of edginess as I tried to put the power down after the apex.

The Viper, inevitably, feels less together, but not perhaps to the extent that reflects the fact that you could buy four for just one McLaren. I enjoyed the GTS-R more, because it, and the circumstances in which I found it, scared me less. Which will I remember more clearly in 20 years? The McLaren, without a doubt.

HENNESSEY VENOM 600 GTS

EXCLUSIVE TOP-SPEED TEST OF THE WICKEDEST STREET-LEGAL VIPER EVER CREATED/by Jeff Bartlett

203 mph! Can you honestly grasp what that level of brutal velocity is like inside a street car? 203 mph. That's a seriously big number, fast enough to leave a stock Viper GTS lagging 16 mph behind like an unwanted calf. The few lunatics brave enough to mash this 602-horsepower Viper's throttle and hang on for the entire top-speed ride should be anointed into the speed-freak hall of fame. In your wake will be a sea of puny-powered underachievers, such as the Ferrari 550 Maranello, Porsche 911 Turbo S, and Corvette ZR-1.

With the unveiling of his unbelievably powerful, Venom 600 GTS, performance maestro John Hennessey has established his place alongside automotive power pirates like Reeves Callaway, John Lingenfelter, and Don Yenko. Entry into this elite club is not easy, but producing a series of street-legal 8.4-liter carbon-fiber-

PHOTOGRAPHY BY PLANET-R/RANDY LORENTZEN & WESLEY ALLISON

bodied, true 200-mph Viper coupes opens a lot of doors.

Carroll Shelby proved three decades ago that Texans like to do things in a big way, and Houston-based Hennessey Motorsports (HMS) is no exception. Since '93, HMS' Viper engine development has outpaced tire technology with its ever-increasing V-10 power output and pushed the outer limits of performance sanity with their turn-key, anyone-with-lots-of-cash-can-buy-one Vipers. Through the years that led up to this ultimate Viper, *Motor Trend* has tested each successive iteration of these extraordinary Venom-badged machines, watching the dyno plot points climb off the graph and the quarter-mile times dwindle in size.

Due to an exhaustive rebuild that includes a stroker crankshaft, the 514-cubic-inch V-10 produces 602 of the smoothest, most driveable horses ever to liquefy tires.

Nearly two years ago, *MT* gathered a cross-section of high-performance tuner cars for a no-holds-barred shootout ("Raw Power" March '96). Hennessey brought to the arid test venue a fire-breathing Venom 600 roadster hissing with attitude. This black-with-silver hellstorm on wheels caused tire meltdown the entire length of the quarter mile, making it a paint-threatening feat to squeeze the best time out of the roadster without kissing the concrete track barriers. The 635 horsepower weren't solely to blame; fault also lay with an overly aggressive 3.54:1 ring and pinion that multiplied power like Stephen Hawking calculating the universe's expansion rate.

"If you look back at the 'Raw Power' article," says Hennessey, "that was a radically fast car, but it was obviously a handful to drive. It was loud and rude, but I have a lot of customers who like that."

Hard numbers from the "Raw Power" test squelched same-year RT/10 figures by 1.2 seconds in the 0-60-mph sprint, and even tromped the significantly enhanced '97 RT/10 with a 0.3-second advantage despite spinning the tires like a greased Dremel bit on hardened glass before forward motion took over. The Venom 600 roadster swallowed the quarter mile in 11.8 seconds at 124.0 mph, slithering wildly on the tarmac the entire 1320 feet. Clearly not a proper car for anyone with the driving acumen of Ed Begley Jr.

"I knew that when we developed the Venom 600 package for the GTS, it had to have a razor-sharp, precise feel to it while still being able to turn the numbers," Hennessey tells us. "Our primary focus with the GTS was to create a significantly better-performing car, a faster car, but in doing so, not to take away from the finesse that the GTS offers over the roadster." HMS could have built an even more outrageous car with the Venom 600 GTS that would buck like a Brahman bull in the castrating chute, but instead took the project in a more refined direction, transforming the coupe into a grand asp-kicking tourer. "Our credo is to offer significant performance increases in the Viper without sacrificing the reliability and driveability issue," says Hennessey.

The heart of any HMS-built car is the engine, which is reworked to extremes directly proportional to the customer's checkbook balance, then returned to its original chassis. The gains are made through time-honored traditions of forcing more air through the powerplant, squirting more fuel into the mixture, reducing internal friction, and fortifying the block to withstand the greater forces.

A basic 510-horsepower Venom 500 GTS package ($9995) includes enlarged throttle bodies, high-flow intake manifold, competition air induction system,

Mild to wild Hennessey power...if you can call any 602-horsepower Viper mild! Hang on for 0-60 mph in

3.7 seconds, quarter-mile times of 11.5 seconds at 129.1 mph, and 0-100-0 mph in 12.5 seconds!

Supple Connolly leather, carbon-fiber instrument bezels, and embroidered race buckets remind of the car's performance pedigree. Far right: John Hennessey at speed in his office.

valvetrain fortification, computer upgrade, 3-inch stainless-steel exhaust system, long-tube headers, 3.54:1 rearend, and silicone spark-plug wires. A set of floormats, valve covers, and exterior badging round out the drool-inducing package. Dig out another $12,000 from the sock drawer and step up to the 550-horsepower Venom 550 GTS engine, adding Venom cylinder heads with three-angle valve job, Extrude-Honed-and-ported intake manifold runners, custom computer programming, and an aggressive camshaft.

Take the engine work $7500 further with the Venom 600 GTS engine upgrade to secure unshakable bragging rights while bringing total output to a smooth 602 horsepower. High-performance rings and engine bearings, forged aluminum pistons, wrist pins, steel connecting rods, and crankshaft round out the internals roster. A completely balanced and blueprinted assembly brings the bored-and-stroked 10-cylinder engine to the next performance plateau, with a surprisingly refined character. Now displacing more than Chris Farley at a Japanese bath house, the 514-cubic-inch aluminum powerplant is dyno-tuned before being released into the unsuspecting free world.

To earn the coveted designation "Venom 600 GTS," the monster motor must be fitted to a coupe shrouded in the all-new VenomAero carbon-fiber body pieces. Designer Steve Everitt has skillfully enhanced the already striking body with a possum-gobbling front air dam with splitter, rear fascia with wide open diffuser, and large "Daytona" spoiler. The tasteful execution of these pieces gives the Venom 600 GTS a look that crosses between stock and the GTS-R, while maintaining its own distinct, modern personality of a full-scale Hot Wheels car. Combined with a carbon-fiber hood, these feather-light components reduce overall weight by about 65 pounds.

In keeping with the corporate edict of building a car as refined as it is powerful, the wing's roof-matching height allows the glass hatch to swing up without interference and permits surprisingly good visibility. For our money, we would forego the ant-scraping front splitter, which is a deletable item. Perhaps the best news is that the exterior-enhancing components are available separately, and they cost less than their respective stock Dodge counterparts, despite being molded from true carbon fiber.

The carbon-fiber theme continues inside as high-tech instrument bezels accent the sophisticated character that oozes from every pore of the Connolly leather interior. Black and red cowhide envelops ultra-supportive Sparco race seats embroidered with Hennessey Motorsports logos. A variety of options can further enhance the interior, from a complete race-ready package (rollcage, fire suppression system, etc.) to a carbon-fiber humidor. Beyond the cabin's striking two-tone appearance, several auditory inputs make it clear that this car is special even from the hip-hugging driver's seat. A tunable exhaust features seven settings, ranging from growling predator to shake-your-neighbors-out-of-bed-to-watch-your-burnout. Even in its quietest mode, the rumbling resonance of 10 cylinders combusting pervades the cockpit in a bombardment of testosterone-laced sound waves. The precision-machined engine idles smoothly, and remains commendably refined as the

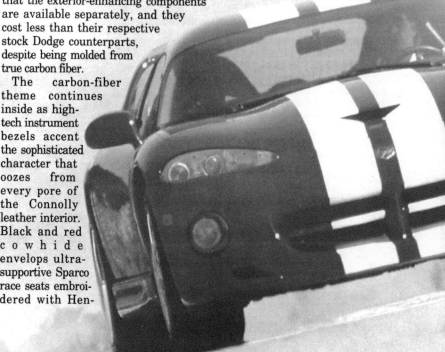

All too often, so-called tuner cars are like hand grenades with their pins pulled. Hennessey

revs climb to the 602 horsepower peak at 5700 rpm.

We began formal testing at a secret 7-mile oval track, with top speed the first order of business. Everyone was at attention as the Venom 600 GTS rumbled at the starting line, anxious to see Hennessey's Viper trounce the 187.3-mph top-speed number of the stock GTS, the fastest production car in America. The thundering coupe blazed off the line and sped out of sight, heading around the town-size track. Before we could down a Lipton iced tea, the Venom 600 GTS flew around the final turn and past our timing traps recording a 203.5-mph top speed. That's 16.2 mph greater than stock, an amazing 34.2 mph faster than a stock (and much more aerodynamic) '97 Corvette, and even faster than the 190-mph Lingenfelter Corvette. Think about it. That's nearly three times most speed limits in the land, and probably double the velocity that Montana state police would let you get away with. Even on a good day.

Despite the challenges in getting a good, clean run from previous over-geared Venom roadsters, the 3.07:1-equipped Venom 600 GTS proved not only to be the fastest street car we've ever tested, but it drove with a mostly controllable demeanor. Launching from the 2400-rpm sweet spot, the Venom 600 GTS ripped a hole through the space/time continuum to swallow the quarter mile in 11.5 seconds at a blistering 129.1 mph.

Once adroitly catapulted off the line, the power curve begins a rapid ascension just north of 3000 rpm, climbing swiftly to the 6200-rpm redline where the infernal power threatens to spin the rear tires even in third gear. The most recent stock GTS to be run through our drill was the fastest virgin Viper we've ever tested (May '97), seemingly blessed by the hand of God. Achieving a 119.3-mph trap speed in the quarter mile in 12.2 seconds, it completely dusted its international competitors in nearly all performance categories in the "High-Speed Gamble" mega-flog, including the new Corvette, Ferrari F355, and Porsche 911 Turbo. Make no mistake: The Hennessey Venom 600 GTS goes one further, picking its fangs with the shriveled egos of dozens of sports cars that now find themselves cowering in the shadow of this new muscle-bound legend.

Three issues ago, we sang praises for the Porsche 911 Turbo S and AutoThority 911 Turbo, a pair of high-tech, twin-turbo coupes that utterly redefine the term "speed." These all-wheel-drive particle accelerators tore down the dragstrip in 11.9 seconds at 116.6 mph and 11.8 seconds at 118.6 mph, respectively. The Venom 600 GTS performs the same stunt several tenths quicker with an over-10-mph-greater terminal velocity. The classic Cobra 0-100-0-mph test had the Venom 600 GTS obliterating the 427 S/C's best by 3.1 seconds—enough time for the cytotoxic Hennessey Viper to accelerate back to 50 mph again!

Rounding out the exorbitant package is a revised suspension using EMI/Penske triple-adjustable shocks with lowered, sport springs akin to units found on Formula One and Indy cars. This permits adjustment of the compression and rebound damping, allowing the car to be

Motorsports backs its full conversions with a 3-year/36,000-mile warranty.

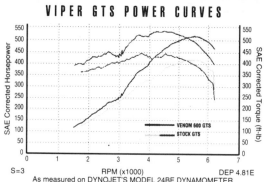

set up specifically for a road course, dragstrip, or the simple ride home. Suspension demon tweaks are certainly possible, but we tested the coupe with its street settings, which proved indiscernible from a stock Viper also at the track. Although production Venom 600 GTS cars will ride on 18-inch Kinesis wheels, our prototype tester had stock-size wheels with factory Michelin rubber. As such, we were not surprised at the similarities in the handling performance compared to a stock GTS. Numbers reveal a 0.1-mph slalom advantage by the bone-stock coupe, but that was the best of several runs. On the other hand, the HMS-built Viper consistently ran at 73.5 mph. Its behavior was relatively forgiving within the context of ultra-high-performance cars and was less treacherous than the non-modified GTS. The slotted Alcon rotors didn't reduce 60-0-mph braking distances, but combined with the brake ducting, they offer day-long, fade-free service. Again, the true benefits are best seen on a race course, where the utterly explosive acceleration as the performance attribute can be savored most often.

Perhaps more surprising than its tectonic-plate-shifting power is the refined character of the Venom 600 GTS. Around town, the 514-cubic-inch engine idles smoothly, refusing to overheat or otherwise misbehave. Under mild acceleration, the car behaves almost benignly, at least within the realm of Vipers. However, a romp on the loud pedal awakens the sleeping beast like a red-hot poker. You'd better be ready for action.

To help ensure there'll be repeat customers, Hennessey provides each Venom 600 GTS buyer with a certificate redeemable for a one-day session at the Dodge/Skip Barber Driving School. The school's use of stock GTS cars makes it the perfect Driver's Ed course for HMS customers.

When John describes the Venom 600 GTS as the "ultimate Hennessey thus far," it begs the question of where to go from here—any more horsepower would be shown with exponents as model designations. The answer is the Venom 600 CS, as in Club Sport. This similar vehicle would focus on further reducing weight by deleting such frivolities as air conditioning and stereo. Lexan would replace side and rear glass, while carbon-fiber doors and underpan would further shave precious ounces and reduce drag. In terms of balance between performance, luxury, and refinement, however, the Venom 600 GTS will reportedly remain the king of all street cars.

As HMS begins to look to modify other new Chrysler models, such as the Prowler and Durango, the speed-addicted company will continue to enhance ownership for all customers, moving Hennessey Motorsports in the direction of an almost Aston Martin-like boutique experience. At present, John ensures each customer receives close, personal attention. Tours of the 14-bay, 30,000 square-foot facility are available, and newsletters keep the growing owner base informed of Viper developments. Future plans include exclusive HMS invitational events that will develop a sense of community—and plenty of friendly rivalry.

Armchair race-car drivers may debate ad infinitum the merits of the Venom 600 GTS versus international starlets such as the Ferrari F50 and Porsche 911 GT1—license-plate-fitted race cars worth more than most executives' retirement accounts. But know this: The GT1 may boast a 0.1-second advantage to 60 mph based on manufacturer claims, but the Venom 600 GTS has a higher top speed than both erotic exotics. And for the price difference, you could have two $150,000 Hennessey cars and a lovely home for the price of either European "supercar."

We have no doubt where our money would be invested.

TECH DATA

HENNESSEY VENOM 600 GTS

GENERAL
Location of final assembly...................Houston, Texas
Body style ....2-door, 2-pass.
EPA size class ....Two-seater
Drivetrain layout......................Front engine, rear drive
Airbag...Dual

POWERTRAIN
Engine type......V-10, cast aluminum block and heads
Bore x stroke, in./mm....................4.01x4.08/101.9x103.6
Displacement, ci/cc 514/8426
Compression ratio...10.0:1
Valve gear ....OHV, 2 valves/cyl.
Fuel/induction system............Sequential multiport EFI
Horsepower, hp @ rpm, SAE net...............602 @ 5700
Torque, lb-ft @ rpm, SAE net....................630 @ 4500
Horsepower/liter...71.4
Redline, rpm 6200
Transmission type...............................6-speed manual
Axle ratio..3.07:1
Final-drive ratio 1.54:1
Engine rpm, 60 mph in top gear 1200
Recommended fuel ....Premium unleaded

DIMENSIONS
Wheelbase, in./mm..96.2/2444
Track, f/r, in./mm....................................59.6/60.6/1514/1538
Length, in./mm...176.7/4488
Width, in./mm...75.7/1924
Height, in./mm..47.0/1195
Base curb weight, lb 3250
Weight distribution, f/r, % 46/54
Cargo capacity, cu ft 9.2
Fuel capacity, gal..19.0
Weight/power ratio, lb/hp 5.4

CHASSIS
Suspension, f/r...............Upper and lower control arms,
    EMI/Penske 3-way shocks, coil springs, anti-roll bar/
    Upper and lower control arms,
    EMI/Penske 3-way shocks, coil springs, anti-roll bar
Steering type ....Rack and pinion, power assist
Ratio 16.7:1
Turns, lock to lock 2.4
Turning circle, ft..40.5
Brakes, f/r............................14.0-inch vented discs/
                                13.0-inch vented discs
Wheels, f/r, in. ....17x10.0/17x13.0, aluminum
Tires 275/40ZR17/335/35ZR17,
                                Michelin Pilot SX MXX3

PERFORMANCE
	Venom 600 GTS	Stock Viper GTS
Acceleration, sec		
0-30 mph	1.6	1.7
0-40 mph	2.2	2.4
0-50 mph	3.1	3.1
0-60 mph	3.7	4.0
0-70 mph	4.4	4.9
0-80 mph	5.1	6.0
0-90 mph	6.4	7.7
0-100 mph	7.4	9.1
Standing quarter mile, sec/mph	11.5/129.1	12.2/119.3
Braking, 60-0 mph, ft	130	129
0-100-0 mph, sec	12.5	13.9
Top speed, mph	203.5	187.3
Lateral acceleration, g	1.03	1.01
Speed through 600-ft slalom, mph	73.5	73.6
EPA fuel economy, mpg, city/hwy	N/A	12/21
Est. range, city/hwy miles	N/A	228/399

PRICE
Base price.................................$150,000 ....$66,000
Price as tested...........................$150,000 ....$73,030

www.hennesseyms.com
www.4adodge.com

Dodge Viper GTS
Big-hearted muscle car is right at home

TWO THOUSAND REVS ON one dial, one hundred em pee haitch on the other. The Viper is relaxing in the sun – well, the eight-litre engine is. The chassis is jumping all over the distressed blacktop and the driver's breathing is becoming increasingly erratic as the twitching reptile slithers between a 300-wheel Peterbilt and a 500-wheel Freightliner.

Exercise fingertip control at the wheel of this car on anything other than the finest freshly-laid tarmac and it will shimmy and bounce and eat away at your confidence until you stop, shoot it full of holes, set fire to it and get on a Greyhound bus. Simply unpop the rhinestone poppers on your heavily embroidered shirt right down past your belly-button to the Colt handguns belt buckle, take another slug from the quart of Wild Turkey, spark up a Winston, grip the big old wheel like a bronco-buster grabs a mustang mane, and y'all will have a good time now.

In the big country, the big, ridiculous car is king. Which is why the Viper doesn't quite make it in Britain where roads are bumpy and, more horribly, narrow; if the Viper jumps direction, you'll be in a grass bank. In America, there's considerably more leeway in highway width and the roadside furniture department, as long as the good 'ole boys are safely tucked up in the truckers' lounge, not giving it tenfourgoodbuddy nose to tail at a million miles an hour.

American cars out of context are largely laughable, but back in their backyard it's a different story.

Comfortably the quickest, comfortably the most comfortable and simply the grooviest of the four, you get more out of America in the big Dodge than in any of the other cars. People talk to you when you bowl up somewhere in a flash car – that's just what happens on the west coast – but in a Viper, folks shout at you from moving vehicles (things like 'asshole' when you break the rules at four-way crossings). 'Hey, slick, I gotta 427 Corvette, shut you down any goddam time you like, so loud they won't let me run it on the strip no more,' from a possible bullshitter in a GMC pick-up, possible because you just can't tell in America if things are for real or not. He might well have had a 427 Corvette, but he could just as easily have owned a 4/27th scale model of a ride-on lawnmower.

Or the ridiculously pretty sandwich girl (you know what it's like when you've been away from womenfolk for days on end) at the Lone Pine truckstop, 'Whoa, Dodge Viper, where you headed guy?' I tell her. 'Way to go, haulin' ass, suckin' gas.' Or how about the charming front desk manager at the super-flash Argyle Hotel, Sunset Boulevard, LA, who begged for a trip round the block, not in the Ferrari, or the Vette, or the NSX, but in the Viper, and she couldn't stop beaming for the rest of the day. This is what the Viper does.

Naturally, this rubs off on the driver, and as you sit behind the seething cauldron of V10, low and long and leaving little tell-tale smears of Michelin Pilot at stop signs, gunning it like a menopausal buffoon down city streets and sitting door ajar, one foot

on the deck like the transparent fraud Warren Oates in his GTO in *Two Lane Blacktop*, you should, by any normal parameters, feel like a clown. But this is America, and this sort of thing is not only allowed, it's encouraged. Rude not to, then.

Driving it out of Yosemite in sleet, guided by useless dipped beam, craning through a misted slit of a windscreen was less good, knowing that it looks faster than it is, simply because when big three-figure speeds are on the menu, the Viper requires a driver of greater skill and nerve than this man who was so taken with the Viper vibe in its natural habitat that no-one else got near the thing for any meaningful length of time.

It fried me in the LA rush-hour, scared me half to death in the wet darkness, and pissed its coolant onto the floor at regular intervals, but I wouldn't have swapped it for the world. A shallow man in a flawed car, maybe, but as far as non-Disney trips in America go, this is surely one of the funkiest.

MARK GRAHAM

ENGINE 7990cc pushrod 20V V10
POWER 450bhp at 5200rpm
TORQUE 490lb ft at 3700rpm
FRONT SUSPENSION Struts, lower control arms, coil springs, anti-roll bar
REAR SUSPENSION Struts, transverse and trailing links, coil springs, anti-roll bar
TYRES FRONT: 275/40 ZR17
REAR: 335/35 ZR17
0-60MPH 4.5sec **TOP SPEED** 170mph
FUEL CONSUMPTION 16.6mpg

DODGE VIPER GTS & RT/10

When the Dodge Viper GTS finally came to market in 1996, it brought with it several features, including a more powerful engine, that could not be had on the roadster. For 1998, all the latest hardware from the coupe has made its way to the RT/10. It becomes a much better—and better performing—car in the process.

The 1996 Viper roadster was a cross between the GTS coupe and the '92-'95 RT/10. It carried the closed car's stiffer chassis, rear-exit exhaust, aluminum suspension components and handsome 5-spoke wheels ... but not the 450-bhp V-10. It had to make do with just 415. This year (actually brought on line as a late-build 1997 model) the transformation is complete; the 8.0-liter 450-bhp V-10 is now the only engine offering for both the coupe and RT/10, and it just makes the Vipers that much faster. A Borg Warner T-56 6-speed manual remains the only transmission offering.

Along with the big bad motor comes a new interior design for the roadster and (can it be true?) roll-up windows. Now if the sports-car purist in you saddens at the thought of something like power windows on a real sports car, forget it. These modern conveniences make the Viper more pleasant and secure. No more fidgeting with side curtains or sliding plastic windows.

Other interior revisions include an adjustable pedal assembly, minor enhancements to the dash and an electronic security system. Yet another first is dual airbags. Considering the size of the car, Dodge has done an admirable job of integrating the system into the Viper; even the airbag-equipped steering wheel is reasonably handsome. It's now possible to actually lock a Viper roadster, and the doors are opened via a nifty solenoid switch-and-grab-handle setup on the doorpost. The sport seats give excellent lateral support for the hard cornering forces you are likely to encounter and are finished in dark gray leather.

A CD player, removable hardtop and a/c are now standard, though the latter two may be deleted for a lower MSRP if desired ($2,500 and $1,000 respectively). Dodge continues to fiddle with the palette of available color combinations. This year, both cars can be had in solid red or the Shelby Cobraesque blue-with-white-stripes combo. The wheels are offered in several different standard and custom finishes, and special-order Viper badging is also available.

All the rest is as you remember it: tubular-steel space frame with center spine structure, resin transfer-molded composite bodywork, fully independent suspension with front and rear anti-roll bars, coil springs, gas shocks, power rack-and-pinion steering, 17-in. alloy wheels and huge 13-in. ventilated-disc brakes.

The Dodge Viper is for the driver who values performance above everything else. If you want a cushy ride, fancy electronic bells and whistles, or wood trim and an automatic transmission, shop elsewhere. Nothing on the market at this price, foreign or domestic, offers the performance to beat it. Now, with enhanced weather protection, security and safety, you can enjoy it that much more often.

QUIKFACTS

MODEL	MSRP	ENGINE	TRANS	ABS	SEATS	A/C
RT/10	est $66,000	V-10	6M	NA	2	STD
GTS	est $66,000	V-10	6M	NA	2	STD

SPECIFICATIONS

Layout	rwd
Wheelbase	96.2 in.
Track, f/r	59.6/60.6 in.
Length	175.1 in.[1]
Width	75.7 in.
Height	44.0 in.[2]
Curb weight	3319 lb[3]
Base engine	450-bhp ohv 20V V-10
Bore x stroke	101.6 x 98.5 mm
Displacement	7990 cc
Compression ratio	9.6:1
Horsepower, SAE net	450 bhp @ 5200 rpm
Torque	490 lb-ft @ 3700 rpm
Fuel econ, city/hwy	est 12/21 mpg
Optional engine(s)	none
Transmission	6M
Suspension, f/r	ind/ind
Brakes, f/r	disc/disc
Tires	275/40ZR-17 (f) 335/35ZR-17 (r)
Luggage capacity	6.8 cu ft[4]
Fuel capacity	19.0 gal.
Warranty, years/miles:	
Bumper-to-bumper	3/36,000
Powertrain	3/36,000
Rust-through	7/100,000

[1] GTS 176.7 in.
[2] GTS 47.0 in.
[3] GTS 3383 lb
[4] GTS 9.2 cu ft
est estimated